FEARLESS FAITH

90 DEVOTIONS for TEENS

FEARLESS FAITH

90 DEVOTIONS FOR

TEENS

Our Daily Bread
Publishing™

Requests for permission to quote from this book should be directed to: Permissions Department, Our Daily Bread Publishing, PO Box 3566, Grand Rapids, MI 49501, or contact us by email at permissionsdept@odb.org.

Scripture quotations, unless otherwise indicated, are taken from the Holy Bible, New International Version®, NIV®. Copyright © 1973, 1978, 1984, 2011 by Biblica, Inc.™ Used by permission of Zondervan. All rights reserved worldwide. zondervan.com.

Scripture quotations marked ESV are taken from the ESV® Bible (The Holy Bible, English Standard Version®), copyright © 2001 by Crossway, a publishing ministry of Good News Publishers. Used by permission. All rights reserved.

Scripture quotations marked NKJV are taken from the New King James Version®. Copyright © 1982 by Thomas Nelson. Used by permission. All rights reserved.

Scripture quotations marked NLT are taken from the Holy Bible, New Living Translation, copyright ©1996, 2004, 2015 by Tyndale House Foundation. Used by permission of Tyndale House Publishers, Inc., Carol Stream, Illinois 60188. All rights reserved.

Interior design by Michael J. Williams

ISBN 978-1-64070-037-6

Library of Congress Cataloging-in-Publication Data Available

Printed in the United States of America

20 21 22 23 24 25 26 27 / 8 7 6 5 4 3 2 1

INTRODUCTION

DISCOVERING FEARLESS FAITH

Katie Davis Majors was an ordinary eighteen-year-old, active in her local church and president of her senior class. Inspired by the love of Jesus, she decided to uproot her life.

Following high school graduation, she moved from Brentwood, Tennessee, to rural Uganda—teaching kindergarten at an orphanage. Moved by compassion for the needs of the orphans she served, she soon began Amazima Ministries, which today educates more than seven hundred children. And by age twenty-three, she had adopted thirteen children who had been abandoned or orphaned.

Katie has a fearless faith. She is not alone. Here and around the world, a generation of teenagers and young adults are being compelled by the gospel to risk their lives on behalf of the oppressed; to address issues like poverty, human trafficking, and the water crisis; and to courageously share the hope they have in Christ Jesus.

Where does that kind of courage start? It begins in *friendship*—a connection with Someone larger than we are, who loves us more than anyone else on the planet, who always wants what's best for us—Jesus, God's Son. When we spend time with Him, when we read the Bible and talk to God in prayer, our courage grows.

That's why we are excited to explore what it means to live boldly for Jesus in *Fearless Faith: 90 Devotions for Teens*. Through reading real-life stories, you will be inspired to pursue your calling, while deepening your relationship with Jesus.

Find a comfortable space to read each devotional. Settle in, getting ready to hear from and talk to God. Read the day's Scripture passage provided here. Most of this devotional uses the New International Version, but you can also read the passage in other versions, either in your own Bible or on a Bible app or website. Then sit with the devotional content, and ask God about His dreams and desires for you—because you have been created *for such a time as this* (Esther 4:14).

JOHN 14:1-12

¹ "Do not let your hearts be troubled. You believe in God; believe also in me. ² My Father's house has many rooms; if that were not so, would I have told you that I am going there to prepare a place for you? ³ And if I go and prepare a place for you, I will come back and take you to be with me that you also may be where I am. ⁴ You know the way to the place where I am going."

⁵ Thomas said to him, "Lord, we don't know where you are going, so how can we know the way?"

⁶ Jesus answered, "I am the way and the truth and the life. No one comes to the Father except through me. ⁷ If you really know me, you will know my Father as well. From now on, you do know him and have seen him."

⁸ Philip said, "Lord, show us the Father and that will be enough for us."

⁹ Jesus answered: "Don't you know me, Philip, even after I have been among you such a long time? Anyone who has seen me has seen the Father. How can you say, 'Show us the Father'? ¹⁰ Don't you believe that I am in the Father, and that the Father is in me? The words I say to you I do not speak on my own authority. Rather, it is the Father, living in me, who is doing his work. ¹¹ Believe me when I say that I am in the Father and the Father is in me; or at least believe on the evidence of the works themselves. ¹² Very truly I tell you, whoever believes in me will do the works I have been doing, and they will do even greater things than these, because I am going to the Father."

IS JESUS EXCLUSIVE?

A famous Christian was being interviewed on television when the interviewer asked, "Are you one of those Christians who believe that Jesus is exclusively the only way to heaven?" He added, "You know how mad that makes people these days!"

Without blinking the woman replied, "Jesus is not exclusive. He died so that anyone could come to Him for salvation."

What a great answer! There's never a reason to argue or fight when we're talking about God. Christianity is not a special club limited to the few people who fit perfectly. Everyone is welcome, no matter who they are, where they come from, or what they have done. Jesus died to pay the penalty for our sins and then rose from the dead. No other religious leader did this, because all other religious leaders are people. Jesus is God himself.

Jesus's words in John 14:6 are not meant to offend but to free: you are welcome here. You matter here. Jesus loves you personally. Jesus sees you. He knows the mistakes you've made and the thoughts you think. He cherishes the good thoughts and dreams. He will help you move away from the destructive thoughts and dreams.

In good times and bad, fun times and fearful, boring times and exciting, the God of the universe cares for you personally!

?

How have you defused an argument about Christianity, Jesus, or God? How does it help to take seriously the questions people ask? How has God helped you work through your own questions?

⁸ If we claim to be without sin, we deceive ourselves and the truth is not in us. ⁹ If we confess our sins, he is faithful and just and will forgive us our sins and purify us from all unrighteousness. ¹⁰ If we claim we have not sinned, we make him out to be a liar and his word is not in us.

FROM MISTAKE TO MASTERPIECE

We all mess up. Whether in big things or little things, everyone makes mistakes. It's what we do after them that really makes the difference. Do we try to hide them? Do we correct them? Do we apologize for them and figure out how to keep from hurting a person that way again? Artist James Hubbell says, "Mistakes are gifts." Whenever he's working on a masterpiece and something goes wrong, he doesn't start over. He looks for a way to use his mistake to make something better.

When we get things wrong, God doesn't throw us away and start over. He redeems us and makes us better. That doesn't mean bad things become good, or that we should try to make more mistakes so we can learn more. It means that each of us is a masterpiece in progress.

The apostle Peter made some huge mistakes. He tended to rush headlong into whatever seemed best at the moment. Sometimes he hit the target. Sometimes he missed by a mile. He was the one who identified Jesus as the Messiah (Mark 8:29). But he later—with sincerity—tried to talk Jesus out of His mission (Matthew 16:21–23). His best-known blunder may have been claiming three times that he didn't even know Jesus (John 18:15–27). If you know the story, you probably remember that Jesus had predicted Peter's denial, but Peter couldn't imagine he'd ever mess up that badly (Matthew 26:33–35). He was wrong.

Did Jesus give up on Peter? No. Peter was willing to learn and grow. In spite of Peter's humiliating denial, Jesus trusted Peter to serve God's people with these words: "Feed my sheep" (John 21:17).

If you have made a mistake so big that it seems irreversible, the most important thing is whether you choose now to show love to Jesus and His people. If you will turn to Him, Jesus will take you from your most serious mistake to create a beautiful masterpiece.

Talk with God about some of the mistakes you've made. Ask Him to work in you to understand His forgiveness and to see how He can use your life for great things.

DAY 3

¹³ Therefore, with minds that are alert and fully sober, set your hope on the grace to be brought to you when Jesus Christ is revealed at his coming. ¹⁴ As obedient children, do not conform to the evil desires you had when you lived in ignorance. ¹⁵ But just as he who called you is holy, so be holy in all you do; ¹⁶ for it is written: "Be holy, because I am holy." . . .

²² Now that you have purified yourselves by obeying the truth so that you have sincere love for each other, love one another deeply, from the heart.

START WITH ONE STEP

What's the most difficult thing you've been told to do? Long division? An essay on Tudor history? To say you're sorry to a sibling? Maybe those things seem too trivial. To keep a secret that shouldn't be kept? To shut your mouth when you want to shout? To stay in the house for days on end without seeing your friends? How about "Be holy, because I am holy"?

What? How can we ever be as perfect, loving, and holy as God? Well, you were made in God's image. So He has given you the raw materials. Also, the command to be holy is in the Bible (Leviticus 11:44; 1 Peter 1:16).

We may never fully understand how we can become more like God. But His promise to us is that, as we listen to the Holy Spirit and let Him lead us, we will slowly grow to be more like Jesus.

Taking one step at a time helps. For example, is there something you know you do, say, or think that doesn't show God's love and holiness? Maybe you're quick to criticize others. Or you have a secret obsession. Or you aggravate your little brother. Tackle that area today. Talk to God about it. Ask for His forgiveness. Then, by His power, start moving on from it.

Step by step, come closer to Jesus and let your life imitate Him. After all, it's not our own holiness we're trying to achieve—we want to live more and more in His!

?

Holy is being like God, so what is God like? Why do you think God wants you to be holy?

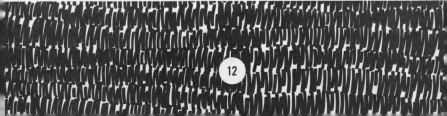

DAY 4

24 "Everyone who hears these words of mine and puts them into practice is like a wise man who built his house on the rock. 25 The rain came down, the streams rose, and the winds blew and beat against that house; yet it did not fall, because it had its foundation on the rock. 26 But everyone who hears these words of mine and does not put them into practice is like a foolish man who built his house on sand. 27 The rain came down, the streams rose, and the winds blew and beat against that house, and it fell with a great crash."

28 When Jesus had finished saying these things, the crowds were amazed at his teaching, 29 because he taught as one who had authority, and not as their teachers of the law.

THE INSTRUCTION MANUAL

Some people love playing board games— the more complicated the better. Opening the box for the first time is part of the excitement. Putting pieces together, examining the intricate details, opening all the plastic-wrapped bundles. And then there are the instructions. Sometimes twenty or more pages of them. Those aren't usually as much fun. Imagine trying to play the game without reading them or without having someone else teach the game to you. It's unlikely you'd figure out the right way to play just by guessing.

It's easy to think that we have no need for instructions for our lives, only to later realize that we've messed things up. Jesus encouraged a countercultural approach—to be bold enough to trust the truth. Jesus gave us the instruction sheets to enjoy a fascinating, solid, and relationship-filled life. We only get one go at this life, so why not do it right?

Today's Bible reading is part of a long sermon Jesus gave that people now call the Sermon on the Mount (Matthew 5–7). Earlier in the sermon, he'd told the crowd to stop the cycle of revenge, go the extra mile for people, forgive enemies, and give up what they had so that they could look out for others first (5:38–44). But just hearing and knowing the instructions isn't enough. The key is to follow them. "Everyone who hears these words of mine and puts them into practice is like a wise man who built his house on the rock" (7:24).

To build a rock-solid and happy life, follow Jesus's instructions. If your foundation is slipping or if you've assembled some pieces wrong, go back to the basics and start over. You'll look much smarter than the ones who set aside the instruction sheet. Those who don't follow the instructions are, as Jesus put it, "foolish" (v. 26). You can stop being a fool, or refuse to start. Courageously read that instruction book!

?

When have you followed one of God's instructions and realized it made you look wise? When have you not followed one of God's instructions and realized it made you look foolish?

PSALM 118:19–24, 29 (NKJV)

¹⁹ Open to me the gates of righteousness;
I will go through them,
And I will praise the LORD.
²⁰ This is the gate of the LORD,
Through which the righteous shall enter.

²¹ I will praise You,
For You have answered me,
And have become my salvation.

²² The stone which the builders rejected
Has become the chief cornerstone,
²³ This was the LORD's doing;
It is marvelous in our eyes.
²⁴ This is the day the LORD has made;
We will rejoice and be glad in it. . . . .

²⁹ Oh, give thanks to the LORD, for He is good!
For His mercy endures forever.

LET'S DO THIS!

A leader opened a gathering by praying, "Lord, thanks for today. It is the beginning of a new day we have never seen before." Although the idea seems obvious, that prayer can help us think about our days a little differently. Imagine praying this the day *before* you learned that school was canceled for the foreseeable future because of a global health crisis. Imagine praying this *on* that day. And on the day *after*. And weeks after that.

Because each day is a new opportunity, it will be filled with some things we can anticipate and prepare for as well as some things we can't. So in both cases it's important that we recognize our limitations and lean heavily on God—actively choosing to follow His direction in whatever comes and relying on His strength.

This prayer also reminds us that the newness of each day is a gift worth celebrating. Perhaps this concept was what prompted the psalmist to say, "This is the day the LORD has made; we will rejoice and be glad in it" (Psalm 118:24 NKJV).

Today may hold joys or difficulties, probably both. Even so, the treasure of each brand-new day is so special that Moses was led to write, "Teach us to number our days, that we may gain a heart of wisdom" (Psalm 90:12).

Every new day is a gift. Ready to take it on? Let's do this!

?

How would you advise someone to take on a new day? How do the good parts of the day help you with the bad parts?

24 Now Thomas (also known as Didymus), one of the Twelve, was not with the disciples when Jesus came. 25 So the other disciples told him, "We have seen the Lord!"

But he said to them, "Unless I see the nail marks in his hands and put my finger where the nails were, and put my hand into his side, I will not believe."

26 A week later his disciples were in the house again, and Thomas was with them. Though the doors were locked, Jesus came and stood among them and said, "Peace be with you!" 27 Then he said to Thomas, "Put your finger here; see my hands. Reach out your hand and put it into my side. Stop doubting and believe."

28 Thomas said to him, "My Lord and my God!"

29 Then Jesus told him, "Because you have seen me, you have believed; blessed are those who have not seen and yet have believed."

30 Jesus performed many other signs in the presence of his disciples, which are not recorded in this book. 31 But these are written that you may believe that Jesus is the Messiah, the Son of God, and that by believing you may have life in his name.

DOUBTS THAT LEAD TO FAITH

Can a believer in Jesus who has doubts about his or her faith ever be effective in serving God? Absolutely. Doubts can be the path to deeper faith when we take those questions directly to God. Some people think that mature and growing Christians never question their beliefs. But just as we have experiences that strengthen our faith, we can also have experiences that cause us to doubt, at least temporarily.

The disciple Thomas had initial doubts about reports of Jesus's resurrection. He was actually smart to investigate rather than to blindly believe. In no part of the Bible is *blind* faith encouraged. Thomas said, "Unless I see the nail marks in his hands . . . I will not believe" (John 20:25). Notice that Jesus did not scold or shame Thomas for his doubts! Jesus showed Thomas the evidence he asked for. And then, amazed at seeing the risen Savior, Thomas exclaimed: "My Lord and my God!" (20:28).

Sadly, many people call him Doubting Thomas. It would be more accurate to call him Trusting-the-Evidence Thomas. We don't know from the Bible what happened to Thomas after this incident, but several early church traditions claim that Thomas went to India as a missionary. These traditions report that while he was there, Thomas preached the gospel, worked miracles, and planted churches. Some of these churches in India still have active congregations that trace their founding back to Thomas.

Let your times of doubt lead to times of discovery. Ask away! By asking, you keep from being taken in by a fake religious group, a false teaching, or a sneaky leader. God will always stand firm. Ask Him anything you want.

?

What are your questions about faith and life and love? Ask God, recognizing that asking is a way to show you trust Him.

[1] After Jesus said this, he looked toward heaven and prayed: "Father, the hour has come. Glorify your Son, that your Son may glorify you. [2] For you granted him authority over all people that he might give eternal life to all those you have given him. [3] Now this is eternal life: that they know you, the only true God, and Jesus Christ, whom you have sent. . . .

[24] "Father, I want those you have given me to be with me where I am, and to see my glory, the glory you have given me because you loved me before the creation of the world.

[25] "Righteous Father, though the world does not know you, I know you, and they know that you have sent me. [26] I have made you known to them, and will continue to make you known in order that the love you have for me may be in them and that I myself may be in them."

Read the whole passage: John 17.

SUNDAY RELATIONSHIP

You sit in the row ahead of Sam in church. You smile and say hi when you spot each other. You say, "See you next Sunday" when you leave. And that's about it. But imagine if one morning you added a little conversation: "Sam, could you give me $100?" or "Would you loan me your car for the week?"

That's kind of like the way we treat God sometimes. We have a friendly, but Sunday-only, relationship with God until we need something. How does that affect God? How does that affect us? Seems like that's using Him, and using someone hurts both sides of a relationship.

God has offered to share with us how to do life, how to get along with friends, how to solve problems, how to find satisfaction. Why would we miss all that by limiting God to Sundays or by keeping our friendship with Him occasional? Why would we treat God like a heavenly vending machine? Why wouldn't we want to get close to Him and listen to His every word?

A 24-7 relationship with God begins when you recognize Him not only as awesome but as your personal Savior. "This is eternal life: that they know you, the only true God, and Jesus Christ, whom you have sent" (John 17:3). Then after you decide to be His child, you let Him be your Lord—the one who has the right to tell you what to do. You let Him show you how to love well during your day-to-day life.

God delights in an ongoing conversation with us throughout each day. While God does answer our last-minute prayers, He also wants us to enjoy His 24-7 companionship.

What is your first response to the God of the universe wanting to do life alongside you? What would your life be like if you let God show you what to do in any situation?

²² Because of the LORD's great love
    we are not consumed,
  for his compassions never fail.
²³ They are new every morning;
  great is your faithfulness.
²⁴ I say to myself, "The LORD is my
    portion;
  therefore I will wait for him."

²⁵ The LORD is good to those whose
    hope is in him,
  to the one who seeks him;
²⁶ it is good to wait quietly
  for the salvation of the LORD.
²⁷ It is good for a man to bear the
    yoke
  while he is young.

²⁸ Let him sit alone in silence,
  for the LORD has laid it on him.
²⁹ Let him bury his face in the dust—
  there may yet be hope.
³⁰ Let him offer his cheek to one who
    would strike him,
  and let him be filled with
    disgrace.

³¹ For no one is cast off
  by the LORD forever.
³² Though he brings grief, he will
    show compassion,
  so great is his unfailing love.
³³ For he does not willingly bring
    affliction
  or grief to anyone.

WHAT IS LOVE?

I just don't love you anymore." How painful! These words break our relationships and attack our dreams. When we get hurt this badly, we often try to protect ourselves by hiding away. We stop letting other people into our lives because they might hurt us as well. This sometimes means that we don't even want to trust God or believe He loves us.

The silly (and hurtful) thing is that love is not something you fall into or out of. Love is not a chair. Love is not the result of an accident. Love is a choice. You choose to do the good and caring action for the sake of the other. When we choose to befriend, date, and marry, we choose to find ways to love a person—every time. Yes, attraction helps a lot, but a relationship based on attraction alone will last about six months (based on one study). Love is a repeated choice, a working together with another thoughtful person to create goodness.

When someone stops choosing to care—or may have never cared—we should look at ourselves through the words of Scripture to see where we've been hard to love. We should determine to be more like Christ. But then we need to see their choice as simply that—their choice. We can commit again to choosing to build relationships with other caring Christians who are also trying to be like Christ.

The amazing thing about God's love is He has chosen to keep loving us. Jeremiah went through intense human betrayal that left him tired and lonely. The people who were supposed to be on his side ignored him when he told them to accept God's love and follow Him. In his darkest time Jeremiah thought about God's never-changing love and wrote, "Because of the LORD's great love we are not consumed, for his compassions never fail. They are new every morning; great is your faithfulness. I say to myself, 'The LORD is my portion; therefore I will wait for him'" (vv. 22–24).

—————— ? ——————

How can you go out of your way today to care for a family member, teacher, or student at your school? Be creative!

²⁶ In the sixth month of Elizabeth's pregnancy, God sent the angel Gabriel to Nazareth, a town in Galilee, ²⁷ to a virgin pledged to be married to a man named Joseph, a descendant of David. The virgin's name was Mary. ²⁸ The angel went to her and said, "Greetings, you who are highly favored! The Lord is with you."

²⁹ Mary was greatly troubled at his words and wondered what kind of greeting this might be. ³⁰ But the angel said to her, "Do not be afraid, Mary; you have found favor with God. ³¹ You will conceive and give birth to a son, and you are to call him Jesus. ³² He will be great and will be called the Son of the Most High. The Lord God will give him the throne of his father David, ³³ and he will reign over Jacob's descendants forever; his kingdom will never end."

³⁴ "How will this be," Mary asked the angel, "since I am a virgin?"

³⁵ The angel answered, "The Holy Spirit will come on you, and the power of the Most High will overshadow you. So the holy one to be born will be called the Son of God. ³⁶ Even Elizabeth your relative is going to have a child in her old age, and she who was said to be unable to conceive is in her sixth month. ³⁷ For no word from God will ever fail."

³⁸ "I am the Lord's servant," Mary answered. "May your word to me be fulfilled." Then the angel left her.

MARY

Throughout history, Mary the mother of Jesus has been held up as a role model. And rightly so! She was singled out by God to give birth to the Rescuer of the world. And she accepted the challenge.

Let's take a look at what it meant for her to say yes to God. Living in a small Galilean village where everyone knew everything about everyone else, she would have to live with the shame of being pregnant without being married. Explaining to her parents and neighbors about the visit of the angel and the Holy Spirit probably didn't help her case. And what about her fiancé, Joseph? What would she tell Joseph? Would he believe her?

In light of all this, her words to the angel Gabriel are amazing: "Behold, I am the servant of the Lord; let it be to me according to your word" (Luke 1:38 ESV). She's not a role model because of who she was but because of how she responded to God. Her response reminds us that we can trust God to help us live out His plans—even if it gets awkward.

What does God have in store for you? It won't be a single big challenge—such as becoming the best football player of all time—although that might be included. It will be a series of challenges, like it was for Mary. Start by obeying what you already understand from the Bible. And then watch as godly character unfolds in you, a character worthy of being a role model.

?

Talk with God about what He wants you to do in the next few hours. Don't get bogged down in the next five or fifty years. How does He want you to grow in your character?

37 On the last and greatest day of the festival, Jesus stood and said in a loud voice, "Let anyone who is thirsty come to me and drink. 38 Whoever believes in me, as Scripture has said, rivers of living water will flow from within them." 39 By this he meant the Spirit, whom those who believed in him were later to receive. Up to that time the Spirit had not been given, since Jesus had not yet been glorified.

REVELATION 21:6

I am the Alpha and the Omega, the Beginning and the End. To the thirsty I will give water without cost from the spring of the water of life.

AVOID DEHYDRATION

Have you ever been dehydrated? If so, maybe you've experienced some of these symptoms: dizziness, disorientation, loss of clear vision, headaches. The bottom line is, being dehydrated feels lousy. And the symptoms of dehydration make it clear—water is vital to our well-being.

Experiencing dehydration can give us appreciation for Jesus's invitation in John 7:37 to come to Him and drink. His announcement was dramatic, particularly in terms of the timing. John notes that it was the last day of a great feast—the annual festival remembering the wandering of the Jews in the wilderness. That festival would finish with pouring water down the temple steps to demonstrate God's provision of water for the thirsty wanderers. Jesus chose that moment to rise and proclaim that He is the water we people so desperately need.

Even drinking once a day, you will still get dehydrated. We need to drink throughout the day even when we don't feel like we need it, and we need to drink even more when conditions are rough. Talking with Jesus is similar—we need to communicate with Him throughout the day and even more when conditions are tough. *Thank you, water of life!*

?

How often do you talk to Jesus on a regular day? What might happen if you started checking in with Jesus several times a day?

PSALM 103:1-14

[1] Praise the LORD, my soul;
    all my inmost being, praise his holy name.
[2] Praise the LORD, my soul,
    and forget not all his benefits—
[3] who forgives all your sins
    and heals all your diseases,
[4] who redeems your life from the pit
    and crowns you with love and compassion,
[5] who satisfies your desires with good things
    so that your youth is renewed like the eagle's.

[6] The LORD works righteousness
    and justice for all the oppressed.

[7] He made known his ways to Moses,
    his deeds to the people of Israel:
[8] The LORD is compassionate and gracious,
    slow to anger, abounding in love.
[9] He will not always accuse,
    nor will he harbor his anger forever;
[10] he does not treat us as our sins deserve
    or repay us according to our iniquities.
[11] For as high as the heavens are above the earth,
    so great is his love for those who fear him;
[12] as far as the east is from the west,
    so far has he removed our transgressions from us.

[13] As a father has compassion on his children,
    so the LORD has compassion on those who fear him;
[14] for he knows how we are formed,
    he remembers that we are dust.

GOOD RIDDANCE DAY

Have you ever heard of Good Riddance Day? It's slowly gaining attention around the world. Inspired by a Latin American tradition, Good Riddance Day is meant to be a day at the end of the year when you say goodbye to the bad stuff you've been through. The idea is that you write down any embarrassing, upsetting, or painful memories from the past year—and then you shred them, burn them, smash them to pieces, or delete them. Whatever way suits you!

The writer of Psalm 103 takes this idea further. More than just saying "goodbye and good riddance" to bad memories, when we confess our wrongdoing to God, He says goodbye and good riddance to our sins! In trying to help us understand God's massive love for us, the psalm writer compared this removal to the distance between heaven and earth (v. 11).

Then he talked about God's forgiveness in a similar way: "As far as the east is from the west, so far has he removed our transgressions from us" (v. 12). *Transgressions* is another word for sins. God's love and forgiveness are infinite and complete. He frees us from the power of our sin and selfishness.

You don't have to wait until the end of the year. Why not make today a Good Riddance Day! Talk to God about all the stuff that's happened and, with Him, throw out the regrets and shameful stuff. God has promised to "trample our sins" and "throw them into the depths of the ocean!" (Micah 7:19 NLT).

How does it make you feel knowing that God infinitely and completely forgives your sins to give you a new start? What attitudes and actions do you need to say goodbye to?

MATTHEW 5:13-16

[13] "You are the salt of the earth. But if the salt loses its saltiness, how can it be made salty again? It is no longer good for anything, except to be thrown out and trampled underfoot.

[14] "You are the light of the world. A town built on a hill cannot be hidden. [15] Neither do people light a lamp and put it under a bowl. Instead they put it on its stand, and it gives light to everyone in the house. [16] In the same way, let your light shine before others, that they may see your good deeds and glorify your Father in heaven."

DOING GOOD

Maybe you've heard these sayings about doing good: "No good deed goes unpunished" and "The good you do today will be forgotten tomorrow; do good anyway." The first one is often true, but we should live by the second one. In the book of Acts, Luke summed up Jesus's time on earth by saying that He "went around doing good" (10:38).

What does the Bible mean when it tells us to do good? Well, we know that the reason to do good is because it works. Good benefits people (Titus 3:8). Jesus did good by teaching, healing, feeding, comforting, and highlighting the good in people. Using Jesus as our perfect example, we try to meet the needs of others. It's a way of seeing and it's very personalized. For example, a surgeon who repairs cleft palates is making certain a child can speak and eat just like other children. That's doing good and healing like Jesus did. A tenth grader who welcomes a ninth grader to high school is making certain that friend-to-be doesn't get lost or laughed at. That's doing good. Talk with God about how He wants you to do good in your situations. Are you supposed to focus on math and science so you can one day create cleft palate repair with no scar? Or are you supposed to welcome a ninth grader? Or both, and more?

Doing good is an adventure! To be like Jesus, ask yourself each day: "What good thing can I do today to make Jesus's love known to someone?" When we do good like this, we will be pleasing God and bringing others closer to Him (Matthew 5:16).

How will you copy Jesus by going about doing good? How do you sense Him doing good through you already?

ISAIAH 42:1-4

¹ "Here is my servant, whom I uphold,
      my chosen one in whom I delight;
I will put my Spirit on him,
      and he will bring justice to the nations.
² He will not shout or cry out,
      or raise his voice in the streets.
³ A bruised reed he will not break,
      and a smoldering wick he will not snuff out.
In faithfulness he will bring forth justice;
      ⁴ he will not falter or be discouraged
till he establishes justice on earth.
      In his teaching the islands will put their hope."

BRUISED BUT NOT BROKEN

Fran's dad left when she was eight, and her mother committed suicide when Fran was fourteen. In her pain, Fran frequently fought with her foster parents, but they never gave up on her. Because of their persistent expression of God's love throughout two long years, Fran decided to trust Jesus.

Fran was bruised, no doubt about it. But she was not broken or snuffed out. Fran experienced, through the love of her foster parents, that "a bruised reed [Jesus] will not break, and a smoldering wick he will not snuff out" (Isaiah 42:3). Fran sees that God has done a great work in her, and she is aware that He loved her through the gritted-teeth support, love, and witness of her new family. Although she repeatedly pushed them away, they continued to show love to her. "I think I must have been a real pain, but they didn't give up on me," she says.

Like Fran, you may have experienced the reality that life on this globe is not fair. Whether circumstances are fair or unfair, we can always choose to receive and show God's love. In telling her story, Fran shares the message of Isaiah to show how God loves her. Isaiah told the Israelites they would lose their homes to the Babylonians and be taken away to a foreign country as prisoners (see Isaiah 39:1–8). Yet through it all, God would comfort them and care for them in their difficulties. Generations later, He would send His faithful Servant, Jesus, who would also care for the scared and helpless, as well as the brave and strong.

Though she walked through great pain, Fran didn't break. She took hold of God's love through her foster parents. We too can trust that God will give us the people we need to help us through.

———————— ? ————————

Talk with God about how to show a bruised person they are cherished rather than discarded. Who does God want you to give attention to at school? At church? In your home? At your job?

DAY 14

1 CORINTHIANS 13:1-8

¹ If I speak in the tongues of men or of angels, but do not have love, I am only a resounding gong or a clanging cymbal. ² If I have the gift of prophecy and can fathom all mysteries and all knowledge, and if I have a faith that can move mountains, but do not have love, I am nothing. ³ If I give all I possess to the poor and give over my body to hardship that I may boast, but do not have love, I gain nothing.

⁴ Love is patient, love is kind. It does not envy, it does not boast, it is not proud. ⁵ It does not dishonor others, it is not self-seeking, it is not easily angered, it keeps no record of wrongs. ⁶ Love does not delight in evil but rejoices with the truth. ⁷ It always protects, always trusts, always hopes, always perseveres.

⁸ Love never fails.

ESSENTIAL INGREDIENT

A Bible study leader asked his group to read 1 Corinthians 13:4–8 out loud swapping the word *Jesus* in wherever it read *love*. No problem. It seemed so natural for them to say, "*Jesus* is patient, Jesus is kind. Jesus does not envy, Jesus does not boast, Jesus is not proud. . . . Jesus does not delight in evil but rejoices with the truth. . . . Jesus never fails." He's our absolute model for how to do life and love. He came to earth and followed His own rules.

Then the Bible study leader instructed his crew: "Now, read the passage aloud and say your name instead of *love*." Everyone laughed nervously. He asked one of the students to start. Awkwardly, the student began saying words that felt so untrue: "*Riley* is patient, Riley is kind. Riley does not envy, Riley does not boast, Riley is not proud. . . . Riley never fails." Take a minute to do that exercise yourself . . .

33

The exercise should make us ask ourselves, *How am I stopping God from showing His love through me? How am I letting God show love through me?* We might be going through all the motions of looking like a good person. But are we really loving? It's not just what we do but how we do it that matters. Talent falls flat when it's arrogant or selfish. Things like speaking well, understanding the Bible, even being generous or serving others—all our actions are worthless if they're not done in love (1 Corinthians 13:1–3).

God wants to show His amazing love for others through you. Do you believe you have the ability to love? You do, because God's Spirit will equip you.

?

Think of an action that you do almost every day. Name one way to do that action without love and one way to do it with love.

JAMES 2:14-26

¹⁴ What good is it, my brothers and sisters, if someone claims to have faith but has no deeds? Can such faith save them? ¹⁵ Suppose a brother or a sister is without clothes and daily food. ¹⁶ If one of you says to them, "Go in peace; keep warm and well fed," but does nothing about their physical needs, what good is it? ¹⁷ In the same way, faith by itself, if it is not accompanied by action, is dead.

¹⁸ But someone will say, "You have faith; I have deeds."

Show me your faith without deeds, and I will show you my faith by my deeds. ¹⁹ You believe that there is one God. Good! Even the demons believe that—and shudder.

²⁰ You foolish person, do you want evidence that faith without deeds is useless? ²¹ Was not our father Abraham considered righteous for what he did when he offered his son Isaac on the altar? ²² You see that his faith and his actions were working together, and his faith was made complete by what he did. ²³ And the scripture was fulfilled that says, "Abraham believed God, and it was credited to him as righteousness," and he was called God's friend. ²⁴ You see that a person is considered righteous by what they do and not by faith alone.

²⁵ In the same way, was not even Rahab the prostitute considered righteous for what she did when she gave lodging to the spies and sent them off in a different direction? ²⁶ As the body without the spirit is dead, so faith without deeds is dead.

WASHED IN LOVE

A small church saw an opportunity to show God's love in a practical way. Adults and teens from the church met at a local laundromat to help sort and pay for the washing of everyone who went in. They met people. They shared conversation. They cleaned and folded the clothes together. And sometimes they even gave hot meals to families struggling to make ends meet.

One church volunteer said the greatest reward was in the "actual contact with people . . . hearing their stories." Because of their relationship with Jesus, these volunteers wanted to live out Jesus's love through their words and actions. And they wanted to build real, meaningful relationships with local families.

James explained that everything we do should result from our relationship with Jesus (James 2:14–16). He taught "faith by itself, if it is not accompanied by action, is dead" (v. 17). When we serve God by looking out for others, we show our relationship with Jesus is the center of who we are (v. 24). Trusting Jesus and caring for people go hand in hand (v. 26). That's fearless faith!

After personally accepting Jesus's perfect love, we can share that love in very practical ways with anyone we meet.

Who are some people you've enjoyed serving? How have you done this in ways that help them rather than draw attention to yourself and in ways that respect rather than embarrass them? What person or group might God want you to serve next?

[5] In the same way, you who are younger, submit yourselves to your elders. All of you, clothe yourselves with humility toward one another, because,

"God opposes the proud
but shows favor to the humble."

[6] Humble yourselves, therefore, under God's mighty hand, that he may lift you up in due time. [7] Cast all your anxiety on him because he cares for you.

[8] Be alert and of sober mind. Your enemy the devil prowls around like a roaring lion looking for someone to devour. [9] Resist him, standing firm in the faith, because you know that the family of believers throughout the world is undergoing the same kind of sufferings.

[10] And the God of all grace, who called you to his eternal glory in Christ, after you have suffered a little while, will himself restore you and make you strong, firm and steadfast. [11] To him be the power for ever and ever. Amen.

SNEAKY TALONS

A rabbit nibbled grass in the yard. He was on the small side, with brown-flecked fur and a cotton puff tail. Suddenly, a hawk sliced through the air as fast and precise as lightning. With talons outstretched, he snatched for his prey. The rabbit, however, recognized the approaching danger and zipped to safety, just inches ahead of the hawk.

Just as the rabbit that spotted its predator found safety, we as Christians need to be watchful so we can escape our enemy. "The devil prowls around like a roaring lion looking for someone to devour"

(1 Peter 5:8). The devil is just plain sneaky, not nearly as obvious as a zooming hawk. He makes wrong look right and darkness look like light (2 Corinthians 11:14). He toys with the truth, twisting it just enough to confuse us (John 8:44). He deceives us again and again, trying a new angle every time we figure him out (Genesis 3:1, 4, 5).

The devil does not appear as a red guy with a pitchfork. If he did, we'd recognize him right away. But he sneaks in, seeking to catch us off guard. He's dishonest—but in ways that look holy (Matthew 4:3, 6, 9). In response, we Christians have to be even sneakier, using alertness, clear thinking, and active readiness to avoid him (Matthew 26:41; 1 Peter 5:8).

And we run (1 Corinthians 6:18; James 4:7)! How will you outsmart the enemy today?

— ? —

Today, watch out for your spiritual predator. What kind of lies is he whispering? How is he tempting you? Resist him, so he won't win. He is not the boss of you!

MATTHEW 4:1-11

¹ Then Jesus was led by the Spirit into the wilderness to be tempted by the devil. ² After fasting forty days and forty nights, he was hungry. ³ The tempter came to him and said, "If you are the Son of God, tell these stones to become bread."

⁴ Jesus answered, "It is written: 'Man shall not live on bread alone, but on every word that comes from the mouth of God.'"

⁵ Then the devil took him to the holy city and had him stand on the highest point of the temple. ⁶ "If you are the Son of God," he said, "throw yourself down. For it is written:

"'He will command his angels concerning you,
and they will lift you up in their hands,
so that you will not strike your foot against a stone.'"

⁷ Jesus answered him, "It is also written: 'Do not put the Lord your God to the test.'"

⁸ Again, the devil took him to a very high mountain and showed him all the kingdoms of the world and their splendor. ⁹ "All this I will give you," he said, "if you will bow down and worship me."

¹⁰ Jesus said to him, "Away from me, Satan! For it is written: 'Worship the Lord your God, and serve him only.'"

¹¹ Then the devil left him, and angels came and attended him.

NO SCRIPTURE TWISTING

The devil came to Jesus when He was tired and hungry. Satan uses the same tactic with us. Waiting for when we're off guard in some way, he offers us quick fixes, easy ways out, and sounds-right actions to make us feel better about doing whatever it is. Jesus shows us what to do about these temptations: throw the Bible at the devil.

The devil practices the un-sacred art of Scripture-twisting: he quotes from the Bible but doesn't say what the Bible says. Tricky! And confusing. Let's see how he did that.

The devil took Jesus to Jerusalem and told him to jump off the temple. Then he quoted Psalm 91:11–12 out of context.

Jesus answered, "It is also written: 'Do not put the Lord your God to the test'" (Matthew 4:7).

Later, the devil took Jesus to a high mountain and offered splendor if Jesus would worship the devil. *Ding ding ding.* Wrong! Jesus reminded him that the Bible says, "Worship the Lord your God, and serve him only" (v. 10).

We can do the same thing. The devil may be smarter than we are, but God is smarter than the devil. The Bible is full of verses about gossip, sex, cheating, slander, lying, arguing, stealing, fighting, and every other temptation. We can use them when we're under attack. As you're reading your Bible, highlight or write down verses to use when you're tempted. Then you'll be ready to throw God's words at the devil!

?

Where do you think the devil will sneak in to try to snare you?

[10] Finally, be strong in the Lord and in his mighty power. [11] Put on the full armor of God, so that you can take your stand against the devil's schemes. [12] For our struggle is not against flesh and blood, but against the rulers, against the authorities, against the powers of this dark world and against the spiritual forces of evil in the heavenly realms. [13] Therefore put on the full armor of God, so that when the day of evil comes, you may be able to stand your ground, and after you have done everything, to stand. [14] Stand firm then, with the belt of truth buckled around your waist, with the breastplate of righteousness in place, [15] and with your feet fitted with the readiness that comes from the gospel of peace. [16] In addition to all this, take up the shield of faith, with which you can extinguish all the flaming arrows of the evil one. [17] Take the helmet of salvation and the sword of the Spirit, which is the word of God.

[18] And pray in the Spirit on all occasions with all kinds of prayers and requests. With this in mind, be alert and always keep on praying for all the Lord's people.

ARMED

The writer of Ephesians, a believer named Paul, had been whipped, beaten, stoned, and imprisoned. He was often hungry, thirsty, cold, or tired. Sometimes people didn't want to listen to him, or didn't believe him when they did listen. Strapping on the belt of truth, the breastplate of righteousness, the shoes of peace, the shield of faith, the helmet of salvation, and the sword of the Spirit allowed Paul to stand against all the lies, guilt, and pain the devil threw at him (2 Corinthians 11:22–28; Ephesians 6:10–17).

Which of Paul's problems can you identify with?

Paul suggests that all believers in Jesus put on this armor of God to stand firm in our daily battles and problems. With God's armor on, we too are fully covered and ready for whatever today brings.

What is this armor? God, who is "my rock, my fortress and my deliverer . . . in whom I take refuge, my shield and the horn of my salvation, my stronghold" (Psalm 18:2), provides this armor. We put it on by immersing ourselves in God's truth, accepting Christ's righteousness, and obediently pursuing God, with faith that He can supply all we need to block what the devil throws at us.

Today might be tough. The next day may be easy. Another day may be agonizing. So make sure you've talked with God, fixed your eyes on Him, and put on the armor He's given you. With God's armor on, you are fully covered and ready for whatever today brings.

_____ ? _____

Which piece of the armor seems most needed for what you are facing in life right now? How would it help you? Why do you need the **whole** armor of God?

PSALM 30:1-12

¹ I will exalt you, LORD,
    for you lifted me out of the
        depths
    and did not let my enemies gloat
        over me.
² LORD my God, I called to you for
        help,
    and you healed me.
³ You, LORD, brought me up from
        the realm of the dead;
    you spared me from going down
        to the pit.

⁴ Sing the praises of the LORD, you
        his faithful people;
    praise his holy name.
⁵ For his anger lasts only a moment,
    but his favor lasts a lifetime;
weeping may stay for the night,
    but rejoicing comes in the
        morning.
⁶ When I felt secure, I said,
    "I will never be shaken."

⁷ LORD, when you favored me,
    you made my royal mountain
        stand firm;
but when you hid your face,
    I was dismayed.

⁸ To you, LORD, I called;
    to the LORD I cried for mercy:
⁹ "What is gained if I am silenced,
    if I go down to the pit?
Will the dust praise you?
    Will it proclaim your
        faithfulness?
¹⁰ Hear, LORD, and be merciful to me;
    LORD, be my help."

¹¹ You turned my wailing into
        dancing;
    you removed my sackcloth and
        clothed me with joy,
¹² that my heart may sing your
        praises and not be silent.
    LORD my God, I will praise you
        forever.

MESSES

When Liz was thirteen, she was arrested, handcuffed, and taken to jail for shoplifting. She was terrified when she realized she had to phone her parents. She explained to her dad and mom what had happened and then said brokenly, "I'm sorry."

After what seemed like forever, her parents arrived to take her home. Feeling awful about the pain she had caused them, Liz braced herself for angry words and punishment. She got neither. Her dad said, "I'm not going to punish you. What you did was wrong, but I think you've been punished enough already."

Depending on your experience with human anger, you may or may not have a clear picture of God's anger. God does not lash out, does not punish with anger, and does not blame you for His feelings. When God becomes angry with us for our wrongdoing, it's because He doesn't want us to be cruel to others. He doesn't want us to make a mess that could have been avoided. He doesn't want us to waste our lives. Even when we deserve our punishment, the Bible tells us, "His anger lasts only a moment" (Psalm 30:5). When we turn back to Him, He forgives us (Jeremiah 31:34; 1 John 1:9).

What about you? Have you been afraid to talk to God and admit to Him where you've messed up? What do you fear? Or do you think He's angry with you even though you've asked for His forgiveness? Read Psalm 30:1–5 again and take it all in. God's anger doesn't last, but His love does. He'll show you how to clean up the mess.

———————— ? ————————

What do you need God to do for you after you've messed up? If you're in a current mess, talk to God about that today.

⁸ Taste and see that the LORD is good;
　　blessed is the one who takes refuge in him.
⁹ Fear the LORD, you his holy people,
　　for those who fear him lack nothing.
¹⁰ The lions may grow weak and hungry,
　　but those who seek the LORD lack no good thing.
¹¹ Come, my children, listen to me;
　　I will teach you the fear of the LORD.
¹² Whoever of you loves life
　　and desires to see many good days,
¹³ keep your tongue from evil
　　and your lips from telling lies.
¹⁴ Turn from evil and do good;
　　seek peace and pursue it.

¹⁵ The eyes of the LORD are on the righteous,
　　and his ears are attentive to their cry;
¹⁶ but the face of the LORD is against those who do evil,
　　to blot out their name from the earth.

¹⁷ The righteous cry out, and the LORD hears them;
　　he delivers them from all their troubles.
¹⁸ The LORD is close to the brokenhearted
　　and saves those who are crushed in spirit.

FOG ON THE WINDOWS

The joy of taking a road trip is seeing the dazzling scenery from the comfort of your car. You get to experience mountain ranges like the Rockies or to wind along California's stunning coastline, all the while staying warm and dry. But at times your view may be blocked: condensation on your windows causes fog to develop on the inside, making you unable to see the gorgeous landscapes. And when it rains, water droplets on the outside of your windows hide the view.

Those two scenarios can help highlight why we sometimes miss life. Sin hides the beauty God generously creates for us. Sometimes our sin is inside—in selfishness we can create a fog that makes us see our preferences as more important than anybody else's, and so we push to get own way. Sometimes sin is outside. The injustice of others hurts us or the people we care about. If we focus on the injustice, like focusing on the rain on the window, we can miss seeing beyond it.

We have to do what we can to stop our own evil and the evil of others. Then we are able to enjoy the beautiful view again.

Where do you need courage to tell the truth, stop a wrong, or start a right? Ask God to give you courage to act.

2 CHRONICLES 20:1-2, 15-17

¹ After this, the Moabites and Ammonites with some of the Meunites came to wage war against Jehoshaphat.

² Some people came and told Jehoshaphat, "A vast army is coming against you from Edom, from the other side of the Dead Sea. It is already in Hazezon Tamar" (that is, En Gedi). . . .

¹⁵ He said: "Listen, King Jehoshaphat and all who live in Judah and Jerusalem! This is what the LORD says to you: 'Do not be afraid or discouraged because of this vast army. For the battle is not yours, but God's. ¹⁶ Tomorrow march down against them. They will be climbing up by the Pass of Ziz, and you will find them at the end of the gorge in the Desert of Jeruel. ¹⁷ You will not have to fight this battle. Take up your positions; stand firm and see the deliverance the LORD will give you, Judah and Jerusalem. Do not be afraid; do not be discouraged. Go out to face them tomorrow, and the LORD will be with you.'"

Read the whole passage: 2 Chronicles 20:1–30.

MANAGE DANGER WITH SKILL

While millions watched on television, Nik Wallenda walked across Niagara Falls on an 1,800-foot wire that was only 5 inches in diameter. He took all the precautions he could. But adding to the drama and danger of both the height and the rushing water below, a thick mist obscured Nik's sight, wind threatened his balance, and spray from the falls challenged his footing. Amid—and perhaps because of—these dangers, he said that he "prayed a lot" and praised God.

47

The Israelites also praised God in the middle of a dangerous challenge: a large group of warriors had gathered to fight them (2 Chronicles 20:2). After humbly asking God for help, King Jehoshaphat followed God's instructions from verses 15–17. He also chose a choir to march out into battle in front of the Israelite army. The worshipers sang, "Give thanks to the LORD, for his love endures forever" (v. 21). As they began to sing, the Lord caused the enemy forces to attack and destroy each other.

This is one amazing event! Of course, we can't just start singing out loud and expect our problems to be solved. This was a specific response to specific instructions. But thanking God for His help and His character in the midst of a challenge can guard our hearts against troubling thoughts. It reminds us of the lesson the Israelites learned: "The battle is not [ours], but God's" (v. 15).

Have you ever asked God for help during a challenge? If so, how did you experience God helping you in your circumstance?

JOHN 15:5-8

⁵ "I [Jesus] am the vine; you are the branches. If you remain in me and I in you, you will bear much fruit; apart from me you can do nothing. ⁶ If you do not remain in me, you are like a branch that is thrown away and withers; such branches are picked up, thrown into the fire and burned. ⁷ If you remain in me and my words remain in you, ask whatever you wish, and it will be done for you. ⁸ This is to my Father's glory, that you bear much fruit, showing yourselves to be my disciples."

UMBRELLA FAITH

You know how brothers are. One brother told his little sister that umbrellas were just like parachutes. He told her that if she jumped off something with one in her hand, she would float down to the ground. All she had to do was "believe." So "by faith" she jumped off a barn roof and knocked herself unconscious, suffering a minor concussion.

Faith is only as good as the object in which it's placed. What God has promised, He will do. But we must be sure to act on His real promises, not something we made up or pieced together from out-of-context snippets in the Bible. Faith, or trusting God, has no power in itself. It only counts when it's based on what God has actually said, not what we think He might or should say. That is wishful thinking—like hoping an umbrella works like a parachute.

Here's an example of what people like to quote as God's promise: "Ask whatever you wish, and it will be done for you" (John 15:7). Sounds great! God becomes our own personal genie. But read the context—in fact, a good guide to understand the Bible is to always read *at least* one verse above and one verse below. The next verse says:

"This is to my Father's glory, that you bear much fruit." Ohhhh! So God is not a genie, but instead this promise is that He will help us in our journey to become more like Jesus and "bear much fruit." This fruit is listed in Galatians as "love, joy, peace, patience, kindness, goodness, faithfulness, gentleness and self-control" (5:22–23 NLT).

Read the verse above and below. That will help you know what God is actually saying.

?

How can you keep from reading into the Bible? How can you tell what it actually says?

PSALM 119:33-40

³³ Teach me, LORD, the way of your decrees,
   that I may follow it to the end.
³⁴ Give me understanding, so that I may keep your law
   and obey it with all my heart.
³⁵ Direct me in the path of your commands,
   for there I find delight.
³⁶ Turn my heart toward your statutes
   and not toward selfish gain.
³⁷ Turn my eyes away from worthless things;
   preserve my life according to your word.
³⁸ Fulfill your promise to your servant,
   so that you may be feared.
³⁹ Take away the disgrace I dread,
   for your laws are good.
⁴⁰ How I long for your precepts!
   In your righteousness preserve my life.

LESSON OF THE HORSE MASK

If you've ever lived near a horse farm, you may have noticed that horses sometimes wear masks over their eyes. And you may wonder, how can they see when wearing them? You could even feel sorry for the horses in this condition. But if you believed the animals were blinded by the masks, you would be mistaken. The masks are made of mesh, so the horses can see straight through them. Flies, which spread eye diseases, can't get past them though. So the masks don't keep the horses from seeing; they keep them from going blind!

Non-Christians often make similar conclusions about the Bible to the one that could be made about those masks. They think of the Bible as something God puts over our eyes to keep us from seeing all the fun we could be having. They feel sorry for Christians because they think God keeps us from enjoying life. But as we saw with those masks, sometimes the reality of a situation is different than it appears. The Bible doesn't keep us from seeing all that is good; it shows us where to find the good. The Bible keeps us from being infected by lies that cause blind living.

The Bible doesn't keep us from enjoying life; it makes true enjoyment possible.

?

When have you felt like God or things you heard from the Bible were trying to keep you from having fun? How does choosing God's way make true enjoyment possible?

LUKE 2:8-16

⁸ And there were shepherds living out in the fields nearby, keeping watch over their flocks at night. ⁹ An angel of the Lord appeared to them, and the glory of the Lord shone around them, and they were terrified. ¹⁰ But the angel said to them, "Do not be afraid. I bring you good news that will cause great joy for all the people. ¹¹ Today in the town of David a Savior has been born to you; he is the Messiah, the Lord. ¹² This will be a sign to you: You will find a baby wrapped in cloths and lying in a manger."

¹³ Suddenly a great company of the heavenly host appeared with the angel, praising God and saying,

¹⁴ "Glory to God in the highest heaven,
    and on earth peace to those on whom his favor rests."

¹⁵ When the angels had left them and gone into heaven, the shepherds said to one another, "Let's go to Bethlehem and see this thing that has happened, which the Lord has told us about."

¹⁶ So they hurried off and found Mary and Joseph, and the baby, who was lying in the manger.

DON'T BE AFRAID

Nearly every time an angel appears in the Bible, the first words he says are, "Don't be afraid!" It's no surprise. When the supernatural makes contact with the natural, it makes sense that people land flat on their faces in fear! In real life, angels are not pudgy cherubs but beings who come in the form of strong men to bring messages from God.

Luke tells us about another kind of supernatural personal appearance. Surprisingly, this appearance didn't seem to frighten anyone. He was talking about God coming to us as a human baby named Jesus. When God came to us in this way, people came near—rather than running away. God's messengers were scary, but God himself was not. What could be less scary than a newborn baby?

On earth Jesus was both God and man. It's hard to wrap our heads around the idea of God getting pimples and feeling nervous about making friends. How could a man born in Bethlehem, who grew up as a carpenter's son, be God's chosen one? But Hebrews 2:17–18 and 4:15–16 assure us that Jesus was human. As God, He worked miracles, forgave sins, conquered death, and predicted the future. For His Jewish listeners, who knew the Old Testament stories of God appearing in terrifying ways, like in a pillar of fire (see Exodus 13:21), Jesus was a surprise.

Why did God become a typical Middle Eastern man? We get a clue in an event Luke records of twelve-year-old Jesus asking questions of the religious teachers in the temple: "Everyone who heard him was amazed at his understanding and his answers" (Luke 2:47). For the first time, ordinary people could hold everyday conversations with God.

Jesus could talk to anyone—His parents, a religious teacher, a poor widow, a friendless woman—without first having to announce, "Don't be afraid!"

?

What do you like about not having to be frightened of God?
How do you respond to God who has come to earth, in skin,
so people can understand Him?

ROMANS 5:1-11

¹ Therefore, since we have been justified through faith, we have peace with God through our Lord Jesus Christ, ² through whom we have gained access by faith into this grace in which we now stand. And we boast in the hope of the glory of God. ³ Not only so, but we also glory in our sufferings, because we know that suffering produces perseverance; ⁴ perseverance, character; and character, hope. ⁵ And hope does not put us to shame, because God's love has been poured out into our hearts through the Holy Spirit, who has been given to us.

⁶ You see, at just the right time, when we were still powerless, Christ died for the ungodly. ⁷ Very rarely will anyone die for a righteous person, though for a good person someone might possibly dare to die. ⁸ But God demonstrates his own love for us in this: While we were still sinners, Christ died for us.

⁹ Since we have now been justified by his blood, how much more shall we be saved from God's wrath through him! ¹⁰ For if, while we were God's enemies, we were reconciled to him through the death of his Son, how much more, having been reconciled, shall we be saved through his life! ¹¹ Not only is this so, but we also boast in God through our Lord Jesus Christ, through whom we have now received reconciliation.

LOOKING FOR A HERO

Who doesn't love superhero films! Kicking back and watching Iron Man, the Black Panther, Wonder Woman, Thor, or Superman saving the day—and sometimes the planet. Many people find it inspiring to watch these people using their special abilities to beat the bad guys and save the helpless.

People love these stories because we all need a hero. Someone to zoom in and rescue us from our problems—our pain, breakups, exam results, illnesses, disabilities, and all sorts of other things. We want someone to bring meaning to our lives, to rescue us from being lost.

Jesus is that hero and much more; He's God! He created the whole universe yet chose to leave heaven to come to earth as a human. He healed people. He calmed storms. He brought the dead back to life. He willingly died on the cross to rescue us from our sins and then rose never to die again so that all who trust in Him can live forever (John 3:16). He did all this while we were still sinners (Romans 5:6–8). He loves us that much.

When we turn our lives over to Jesus, He not only saves and rescues us but also continues to be active in our lives, giving us the Holy Spirit's power we need to face anything. We can boast about Him!

What's the most impressive thing about God that you can think of? Share that with someone today.

⁶ Go to the ant, you sluggard;
　　　consider its ways and be wise!
⁷ It has no commander,
　　　no overseer or ruler,
⁸ yet it stores its provisions in summer
　　　and gathers its food at harvest.

⁹ How long will you lie there, you sluggard?
　　　When will you get up from your sleep?
¹⁰ A little sleep, a little slumber,
　　　a little folding of the hands to rest—
¹¹ and poverty will come on you like a thief
　　　and scarcity like an armed man.

BE PREPARED

Do you know how many rolls of toilet paper you have in your house right now? If you don't, someone in your house probably knows.

During one of the most difficult times in our nation's history, the coronavirus pandemic, a tiny bit of humor appeared when many people decided that their most important need through this frightening time was toilet paper. So they stockpiled it, triggering the Great Toilet Paper Crisis of 2020. Stores ran out. People fought over it. And we all wondered, *Why are people doing this?*

It was because they wanted to be prepared. They didn't want to run out of TP when they were kept in their homes by the virus.

While some may have carried this tissue issue to an extreme, it is good to be prepared. In fact, the Bible talks about planning ahead.

In Proverbs, the writer uses the lowly ant to teach this. He said, "Go to the ant, you sluggard; consider its ways and be wise! . . . It stores its provisions in summer and gathers its food at harvest." All those busy little guys you see on your sidewalk are getting ready for winter. Looking to the future, like planning for college or preparing for a job, is a good thing.

In the New Testament we see a much more serious reason to be prepared. Jesus told us to be ready for the time of His return from heaven. In Matthew 24:44, He said, "So you also must be ready, because the Son of Man [Jesus] will come at an hour when you do not expect him." We need to make sure we have put our trust in Jesus Christ as Savior to be ready for His return.

Planning for the future? Put your faith in Jesus. It's the best way to be prepared.

What fears do you have about the future? Talk to God about those fears and ask Him to help you plan for an exciting, joy-filled future.

[31] Again his Jewish opponents picked up stones to stone him, [32] but Jesus said to them, "I have shown you many good works from the Father. For which of these do you stone me?"

[33] "We are not stoning you for any good work," they replied, "but for blasphemy, because you, a mere man, claim to be God."

[34] Jesus answered them, "Is it not written in your Law, 'I have said you are "gods"'? [35] If he called them 'gods,' to whom the word of God came—and Scripture cannot be set aside—[36] what about the one whom the Father set apart as his very own and sent into the world? Why then do you accuse me of blasphemy because I said, 'I am God's Son'? [37] Do not believe me unless I do the works of my Father. [38] But if I do them, even though you do not believe me, believe the works, that you may know and understand that the Father is in me, and I in the Father." [39] Again they tried to seize him, but he escaped their grasp.

[40] Then Jesus went back across the Jordan to the place where John had been baptizing in the early days. There he stayed, [41] and many people came to him. They said, "Though John never performed a sign, all that John said about this man was true." [42] And in that place many believed in Jesus.

MIRACLES OR MAGIC TRICKS?

Did Jesus really walk on water or simply find well-placed sandbars? Did He actually feed more than five thousand people with one boy's lunch, or did He trick the crowd into thinking He did? Did He really bring people back to life, or did He hire them as assistants for His grand performances? Did He do miracles or magic?

When Christian illusionist Brock Gill explored this question for a television broadcast, he reexamined biblical miracles with an open mind. Gill knows illusions so he can recognize a real miracle when he sees one. The show's producer said, "Even if an atheist had been chosen as host, the conclusions wouldn't have changed." In every case, Gill gave evidence why Jesus could not have tricked people into believing they had seen a miracle.

Even with such clear evidence, some first-person witnesses to Jesus's miracles still refused to believe that He really was God. They were ready to kill Him for claiming to be God. They would not consider that He truly was God (John 10:30–31). The miracles themselves served as the evidence in these cases. Jesus told them, "Do not believe me unless I do the works of my Father. But if I do them, even though you do not believe me, believe the works, that you may know and understand that the Father is in me, and I in the Father" (vv. 37–38).

The stories of Jesus are not fairy tales but the truth of God at work on earth. The miracles of Jesus show He really is God. Because He is God we can trust Him to tell us what to do. We can trust Him as our Savior and Lord. Believe based on the evidence.

Why do miracles matter? Which of Jesus's miracles impresses you most?

[1] Therefore, rid yourselves of all malice and all deceit, hypocrisy, envy, and slander of every kind. [2] Like newborn babies, crave pure spiritual milk, so that by it you may grow up in your salvation, [3] now that you have tasted that the Lord is good.

[4] As you come to him, the living Stone—rejected by humans but chosen by God and precious to him—[5] you also, like living stones, are being built into a spiritual house to be a holy priesthood, offering spiritual sacrifices acceptable to God through Jesus Christ. [6] For in Scripture it says:

> "See, I lay a stone in Zion,
>   a chosen and precious cornerstone,
> and the one who trusts in him
>   will never be put to shame."

[7] Now to you who believe, this stone is precious. But to those who do not believe,

> "The stone the builders rejected
>   has become the cornerstone,"

[8] and,

> "A stone that causes people to stumble
>   and a rock that makes them fall."

They stumble because they disobey the message—which is also what they were destined for.

[9] But you are a chosen people, a royal priesthood, a holy nation, God's special possession, that you may declare the praises of him who

called you out of darkness into his wonderful light. [10] Once you were not a people, but now you are the people of God; once you had not received mercy, but now you have received mercy.

INDESTRUCTIBLE

All around London are statues and other items made from a special building material called Coade stone. Created by Eleanor Coade for her family business in the late 1700s, this fake stone is nearly indestructible! Coade stone stopped being used in the 1840s following Eleanor's death, but many examples of this sturdy stone have kept standing against every weather and pollution for over 150 years.

Peter described Jesus as a living stone. He wrote that we stand on this sturdy stone as we rid ourselves "of all malice and all deceit, hypocrisy, envy, and slander of every kind" (1 Peter 2:1). When we experience this way of living, we discover that "the Lord is good" (v. 3).

Jesus is the stone that lasts forever—we can build our lives safely on Him. If He is our strength, we'll be able to keep standing through both stormy and sunny situations, through everything this crazy world throws our way!

When have you had to rely on God's strength to get you through a challenging circumstance? What did that experience teach you?

PSALM 46:1-3

¹ God is our refuge and strength,
   an ever-present help in trouble.
² Therefore we will not fear, though the earth give way
   and the mountains fall into the heart of the sea,
³ though its waters roar and foam
   and the mountains quake with their surging.

2 TIMOTHY 3:10-17

¹⁰ You [Timothy], however, know all about my [the apostle Paul's] teaching, my way of life, my purpose, faith, patience, love, endurance, ¹¹ persecutions, sufferings—what kinds of things happened to me in Antioch, Iconium and Lystra, the persecutions I endured. Yet the Lord rescued me from all of them. ¹² In fact, everyone who wants to live a godly life in Christ Jesus will be persecuted, ¹³ while evildoers and impostors will go from bad to worse, deceiving and being deceived. ¹⁴ But as for you, continue in what you have learned and have become convinced of, because you know those from whom you learned it, ¹⁵ and how from infancy you have known the Holy Scriptures, which are able to make you wise for salvation through faith in Christ Jesus. ¹⁶ All Scripture is God-breathed and is useful for teaching, rebuking, correcting and training in righteousness, ¹⁷ so that the servant of God may be thoroughly equipped for every good work.

BRING IT ON!

Have you ever heard people suggest that if you just trust Jesus, all your problems will go away and life will be easy? That you'll have everything you want and nothing will harm you? Not true!

All of life is hard on this bent planet of ours. We all struggle in some way. Cancer, gossip, COVID-19, disabilities, abuse, persecution—these hurt everyone, whether they have trusted in Jesus or not.

After Paul met Jesus for himself, he trusted Him, and then went through a series of struggles. *Huge* struggles. Paul was fully committed to God, and that actually seemed to make his life *more* difficult (see 2 Corinthians 11:23–33). He told everyone he met about Jesus—and what did he get for his efforts? He was beaten, arrested, shipwrecked, and chased out of cities, to name a few.

So why be a Christian when we face the same problems as everyone else? What difference does it make? The difference is in what we know to be true, that we have learned from the Bible: we have insider information! The Holy Spirit will help us understand and remember (John 14:26) that the all-loving God of the universe will never leave us to struggle alone (Hebrews 13:5–6), and that through Jesus Christ, no matter what happens in this world, we have the confidence of eternal life (1 John 5:13). We don't have to be happy about what happens, but it doesn't have to defeat us or define us.

What's scary to you about problems that you have now or that may come in the future? What truths from the Bible give you comfort and hope?

JOHN 12:12-13

[12] The next day the great crowd that had come for the festival heard that Jesus was on his way to Jerusalem. [13] They took palm branches and went out to meet him, shouting,

"Hosanna!"
"Blessed is he who comes in the name of the Lord!"
"Blessed is the king of Israel!"

JOHN 13:34-38

[34] "A new command I give you: Love one another. As I have loved you, so you must love one another. [35] By this everyone will know that you are my disciples, if you love one another."

[36] Simon Peter asked him, "Lord, where are you going?"

Jesus replied, "Where I am going, you cannot follow now, but you will follow later."

[37] Peter asked, "Lord, why can't I follow you now? I will lay down my life for you."

[38] Then Jesus answered, "Will you really lay down your life for me? Very truly I tell you, before the rooster crows, you will disown me three times!"

JOHN 19:14-16

[14] It was the day of Preparation of the Passover; it was about noon.

"Here is your king," Pilate said to the Jews.

[15] But they shouted, "Take him away! Take him away! Crucify him!"

"Shall I crucify your king?" Pilate asked.

"We have no king but Caesar," the chief priests answered.

[16] Finally Pilate handed him over to them to be crucified.

FICKLE FOLLOWERS

Our images and reputations can yo-yo. When Jesus entered Jerusalem for a feast called the Passover, He was welcomed by crowds willing to lay their coats in the road for Jesus to walk on, cheering to have Him made king (Matthew 21:8). But by the end of the week, the crowds were demanding that He be crucified (John 19:15).

We can recognize ourselves in those fickle crowds. Some of us love cheering for a team that's winning, but our interest fades when they start losing. We love being part of a movement that is new and exciting, but when something is demanded of us, we're often ready to move on. We love following Jesus when He is doing the impossible, but we can slink away when He expects us to do something difficult. It's exciting to follow Jesus when He outsmarts the people in power (see Matthew 22:15–46). But when He begins to talk about suffering and sacrifice, we may hesitate.

Even Peter, one of his closest friends and followers, found it difficult to stand firm under pressure. He wavered, but then recommitted his life fully to following Jesus.

Would we have followed Jesus all the way to the cross? It's hard to know. But we can celebrate that Jesus, through His Holy Spirit, is working to make us brave, so we can become radical followers.

?

Who is someone with a radical faith? What about his or her faith inspires you?

PSALM 22:1-5, 19-26

¹ My God, my God, why have you
forsaken me?
Why are you so far from saving
me,
so far from my cries of anguish?
² My God, I cry out by day, but you
do not answer,
by night, but I find no rest.

³ Yet you are enthroned as the Holy
One;
you are the one Israel praises.
⁴ In you our ancestors put their trust;
they trusted and you delivered
them.
⁵ To you they cried out and were
saved;
in you they trusted and were not
put to shame. . . .

¹⁹ But you, LORD, do not be far from
me.
You are my strength; come
quickly to help me.
²⁰ Deliver me from the sword,
my precious life from the power
of the dogs.

²¹ Rescue me from the mouth of the
lions;
save me from the horns of the
wild oxen.

²² I will declare your name to my
people;
in the assembly I will praise you.
²³ You who fear the LORD, praise him!
All you descendants of Jacob,
honor him!
Revere him, all you descendants
of Israel!
²⁴ For he has not despised or scorned
the suffering of the afflicted one;
he has not hidden his face from him
but has listened to his cry for
help.

²⁵ From you comes the theme of my
praise in the great assembly;
before those who fear you I will
fulfill my vows.
²⁶ The poor will eat and be satisfied;
those who seek the LORD will
praise him—
may your hearts live forever!

IGNORED?

Psalm 22 begins with these heartbreaking words, "My God, my God, why have you forsaken me?" How bad must the situation have been that David, the psalm writer, cried out to God in this way? He felt abandoned: "Why are you so far from saving me?" (v. 1). He felt ignored: "My God, I cry out by day, but you do not answer, by night, but I find no rest" (v. 2).

Ever been there? Have you ever looked up to the sky and asked God why He was ignoring you? We can do what David did: Even feeling abandoned and ignored, David mixed his painful cries with good things about God. That stops us from losing hope. Through it all, like David, you can affirm that God is king (v. 3), that you can trust Him (vv. 4–5), that He'll show you what to do in the worst of the worst times and the best of the best times (vv. 20–21), that God is your strength (v. 19), and that God has definitely not abandoned you (v. 24).

When you and I feel like God's forgotten about us, we have still another source of help: Jesus himself. He spoke these same words on the cross: "My God, my God, why have you forsaken me?" (Matthew 27:46). He knows the feeling. As Hebrews 2:17 explains, He is like us in every way. He gets us. He's been there. And we can approach Him with confidence (Hebrews 4:15–16).

Read the verses from Psalm 22 again, and as you remember who God is, let your heart "rejoice with everlasting joy" (v. 26 NLT).

Begin a conversation with God using these starter words:
God, sometimes I feel as if you don't care about my life.
When those times come, please help me to trust you again
and know you are there . . .

[1] As for you, you were dead in your transgressions and sins, [2] in which you used to live when you followed the ways of this world and of the ruler of the kingdom of the air, the spirit who is now at work in those who are disobedient. [3] All of us also lived among them at one time, gratifying the cravings of our flesh and following its desires and thoughts. Like the rest, we were by nature deserving of wrath. [4] But because of his great love for us, God, who is rich in mercy, [5] made us alive with Christ even when we were dead in transgressions—it is by grace you have been saved. [6] And God raised us up with Christ and seated us with him in the heavenly realms in Christ Jesus, [7] in order that in the coming ages he might show the incomparable riches of his grace, expressed in his kindness to us in Christ Jesus. [8] For it is by grace you have been saved, through faith—and this is not from yourselves, it is the gift of God—[9] not by works, so that no one can boast. [10] For we are God's handiwork, created in Christ Jesus to do good works, which God prepared in advance for us to do.

NOT ONE but TWO SAFETY HARNESSES

Have you ever desired to go bungee jumping? It sounds both fascinating and terrifying. When you bungee jump, you lunge headfirst from a bridge hundreds of feet in the air suspended only by a giant rubber band. But you have support when you leap. You get not one but two heavy-duty harnesses that secure you to your lifeline—and to safety. The careful design and testing of those harnesses should give you confidence as you jump into the air.

For followers of Christ, staying intact in a sinful world is not a blind leap of faith. We too have a pair of protections that can secure us in even the darkest times of life. In Ephesians 2:8–9 Paul wrote these words, "For it is by grace you have been saved, through faith—and this is not from yourselves, it is the gift of God—not by works, so that no one can boast."

It's in these twin harnesses—God's gracious love for us when we didn't deserve it plus faith in the sacrifice of Jesus for our sins—that our relationship with God safely rests. Because we have these promises from God, following Jesus is not a risky leap into the void. It's an exercise of confidence in God's Word and His unfailing love and protection for us.

?

If you have accepted Jesus as your Savior, how does that security help you when life is scary or difficult? If you have not, what's stopping you from making that leap?

[11] Therefore, remember that formerly you who are Gentiles by birth and called "uncircumcised" by those who call themselves "the circumcision" (which is done in the body by human hands)— [12] remember that at that time you were separate from Christ, excluded from citizenship in Israel and foreigners to the covenants of the promise, without hope and without God in the world. [13] But now in Christ Jesus you who once were far away have been brought near by the blood of Christ.

[14] For he himself is our peace, who has made the two groups one and has destroyed the barrier, the dividing wall of hostility, [15] by setting aside in his flesh the law with its commands and regulations. His purpose was to create in himself one new humanity out of the two, thus making peace, [16] and in one body to reconcile both of them to God through the cross, by which he put to death their hostility. [17] He came and preached peace to you who were far away and peace to those who were near. [18] For through him we both have access to the Father by one Spirit.

A PRIZE FOR PEACE

Alfred Nobel was a Swedish chemist, engineer, and industrialist who invented dynamite. His original purpose appears to have been to increase safety at construction sites while blasting rock. But dynamite changed warfare. Perhaps because of the horrors that warriors inflicted with dynamite, Nobel created what's now the Nobel Peace Prize—a cash prize given each year to those who promote peace.

God gives an even more powerful peace. God showed it through coming to live with us. Angels testified to it. Sin threatens it. Good friendships, marriages, and teen-parent relationships deepen it.

People crave peace. At first we think peace is the lack of fighting—whether between two people or several nations. But discord can still exist even with no outward fighting. You've probably felt that icy silence before.

So what is peace, and how do we get it? First it comes through Jesus Christ: when God came to earth in Jesus, the angels' unmistakable message to the shepherds was "glory to God in the highest heaven, and on earth peace to those on whom his favor rests" (Luke 2:14). So peace is first peace with God. Then it is the expression of this peace God has given us (Philippians 4:7). There are different ways we can express peace in our own lives: talking things out honestly and with love, listening to everyone's ideas, valuing each person, and showing interest in others.

You can create peace even more valuable than a Nobel Peace Prize winner.

When have you felt at peace? What led to your feeling of peace?

¹⁸ For through him [Jesus] we both have access to the Father by one Spirit.
¹⁹ Consequently, you are no longer foreigners and strangers, but fellow citizens with God's people and also members of his household, ²⁰ built on the foundation of the apostles and prophets, with Christ Jesus himself as the chief cornerstone. ²¹ In him the whole building is joined together and rises to become a holy temple in the Lord. ²² And in him you too are being built together to become a dwelling in which God lives by his Spirit.

STEADY, STEADY

Plymouth Rock is a well-known landmark thought to be the place where early travelers to America first set foot. If you ever go to visit it, you may be surprised at how small it is! Harsh weather (and people chipping bits off) has left the stone just a third of its original size!

The Bible sometimes speaks about Jesus as a rock who never changes (1 Corinthians 10:4; Hebrews 13:8). The church is built on "Christ Jesus himself as the chief cornerstone," and He is the platform on which all Christians are joined together in a forever-sturdy structure (Ephesians 2:20–22). You are part of a steady, steady structure. You have a forever place of belonging.

Unlike Plymouth Rock, Jesus is much bigger than we expect. We are built on Him as our foundation. We all have the same rock and the same strength—and it's great to be able to remind each other of that truth!

Plymouth Rock has an interesting history, but it's slowly fading away. Jesus is as solid as ever: He'll never disappear. He is the one thing that all Christians have in common, no matter what our ages, nationalities, or backgrounds. We are built on the foundation of Jesus Christ, held up by the Father, and filled by the Spirit. That will keep us steady!

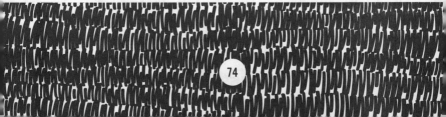

What situations or interactions throw you off balance? Talk with Jesus—who is steady and never changes—about them.

²⁷ Why do you complain, Jacob?
   Why do you say, Israel,
"My way is hidden from the Lord;
   my cause is disregarded by my God"?
²⁸ Do you not know?
   Have you not heard?
The Lord is the everlasting God,
   the Creator of the ends of the earth.
He will not grow tired or weary,
   and his understanding no one can fathom.
²⁹ He gives strength to the weary
   and increases the power of the weak.
³⁰ Even youths grow tired and weary,
   and young men stumble and fall;
³¹ but those who hope in the Lord
   will renew their strength.
They will soar on wings like eagles;
   they will run and not grow weary,
   they will walk and not be faint.

ONE FOOT IN FRONT OF THE OTHER

What's the hardest thing about waiting? Often, it's the not knowing. Like waiting to find out how you did on an exam; or waiting to hear back from the college you want to get into; or even waiting for a reply from a friend you just texted! Will that friend understand what you were trying to say? Or will things get worse? When we're waiting, it can be difficult to relax or even concentrate. Waiting is hard!

But we have to concentrate, and we have to keep going during the wait. There are a dozen things still needing our attention—spending time with God, keeping up with schoolwork, serving others, preparing for the competition, doing chores, practicing an instrument, eating right, checking in with friends, helping siblings, taking care of pets, and on and on.

It's then that Isaiah 40:29–31 means the most: God "gives strength to the weary and increases the power of the weak. Even youths grow tired and weary, and young men stumble and fall; but those who hope in the LORD will renew their strength. They will soar on wings like eagles; they will run and not grow weary, they will walk and not be faint."

Some days all we can do is put one foot in front of the other—to walk and not faint. So we will depend on God to give us the strength to keep going.

?

What is something you've had to wait for—or maybe you're still waiting for? What has the waiting taught you?

17 Though the fig tree does not bud
    and there are no grapes on the vines,
though the olive crop fails
    and the fields produce no food,
though there are no sheep in the pen
    and no cattle in the stalls,
18 yet I will rejoice in the LORD,
    I will be joyful in God my Savior.

19 The Sovereign LORD is my strength;
    he makes my feet like the feet of a deer,
    he enables me to tread on the heights.

THREE-LETTERED FAITH

Do you know any pessimists? You know, the kind of person who quickly jumps to negative conclusions about how things in life will play out. For instance, someone is struggling to complete an assignment and starts assuming that nothing else he or she does is any good either. And suddenly that person thinks, *I'm an awful person who can't do anything right.*

It's easy to imagine how the prophet Habakkuk could have been pessimistic. He might have reacted to what God showed him. He had good reason to give up after God showed him the coming troubles for his people. These problems would last for years. Things really did look bad: no fruit, no meat, and no comfort. Notice Habakkuk's "though the" prayers: "Though the . . . fields produce no food . . ." (Habakkuk 3:17). That sounds like a downer until he surprises us with a small three-letter word: *yet.* "Yet I will rejoice in the LORD" (v. 18). Despite all the hardships he knew were coming, Habakkuk found reason for rejoicing simply because of who God is.

We sometimes overreact or make our problems out to be worse than they are—but Habakkuk's problems were actually bad. Since Habakkuk chose to still walk with God in that journey, we can choose to trust God too. Simple logic lets us know it's wiser to tackle our troubles with God's help rather than all alone.

Write your own "though the" prayer with both scary and happy events. For example, "Though I don't make the team . . ." and "Though I do well on the test . . ." Then write your "yet . . ."

1 JOHN 5:10-15

¹⁰ Whoever believes in the Son of God accepts this testimony. Whoever does not believe God has made him out to be a liar, because they have not believed the testimony God has given about his Son. ¹¹ And this is the testimony: God has given us eternal life, and this life is in his Son. ¹² Whoever has the Son has life; whoever does not have the Son of God does not have life.

¹³ I write these things to you who believe in the name of the Son of God so that you may know that you have eternal life. ¹⁴ This is the confidence we have in approaching God: that if we ask anything according to his will, he hears us. ¹⁵ And if we know that he hears us—whatever we ask—we know that we have what we asked of him.

KNOWING THE FINAL SCORE

Watching your favorite sports team play can be a nerve-wracking experience. Because one goal or mistake in sports like soccer or basketball can change the game, it's easy to feel tense as you watch. But that's also part of what makes the games enjoyable. What if you watched a game already knowing its outcome? You'd feel a lot calmer (and you may be bored)!

Life is often like watching live sports. There are shocks and surprises, frustrations and fears, because we don't know what will happen. Sometimes that's part of the fun. But at other times, we just want to know the ending. Followers of Jesus can relax a bit though—even though many things in life are uncertain, we know we will be safe with Jesus at the end. His death and resurrection have made our future safe and secure! We know how everything's going to end.

John wrote, "I write these things to you who believe in the name of the Son of God so that you may know that you have eternal life" (1 John 5:13). Life may have surprises along the way, but because of our certain future with Jesus, we can have peace.

—————————— ? ——————————

What are some things that cause you anxiety? Talk with God about your anxieties and everyday concerns.

¹ Therefore, since through God's mercy we [Paul and others] have this ministry, we do not lose heart. ² Rather, we have renounced secret and shameful ways; we do not use deception, nor do we distort the word of God. On the contrary, by setting forth the truth plainly we commend ourselves to everyone's conscience in the sight of God. ³ And even if our gospel is veiled, it is veiled to those who are perishing. ⁴ The god of this age has blinded the minds of unbelievers, so that they cannot see the light of the gospel that displays the glory of Christ, who is the image of God. ⁵ For what we preach is not ourselves, but Jesus Christ as Lord, and ourselves as your servants for Jesus' sake. ⁶ For God, who said, "Let light shine out of darkness," made his light shine in our hearts to give us the light of the knowledge of God's glory displayed in the face of Christ.

⁷ But we have this treasure in jars of clay to show that this all-surpassing power is from God and not from us. ⁸ We are hard pressed on every side, but not crushed; perplexed, but not in despair; ⁹ persecuted, but not abandoned; struck down, but not destroyed. ¹⁰ We always carry around in our body the death of Jesus, so that the life of Jesus may also be revealed in our body. ¹¹ For we who are alive are always being given over to death for Jesus' sake, so that his life may also be revealed in our mortal body. ¹³ So then, death is at work in us, but life is at work in you.

FEARLESS SERVICE

Gladys Aylward had big dreams. While serving as a maid in London in the early part of the twentieth century, she knew she was called to be a missionary to China. But when she applied to go to China, a Christian missionary organization rejected her as "unqualified."

Fearless, Gladys decided to go to China on her own. At twenty-eight, she used her life savings to buy a one-way ticket to Yangcheng, a remote village in China. There she set up an inn for trade caravans through which she shared Bible stories. Gladys served in other villages as well and became known as Ai-weh-deh, Chinese for "virtuous one."

The apostle Paul also spread the gospel through traveling to other regions of the world and finding creative approaches. He worked as a tentmaker. He debated the truth in public places. In these and other situations where he met the needs of others, Paul wrote this about serving: "What we preach is not ourselves, but Jesus Christ as Lord, and ourselves as your servants for Jesus' sake" (2 Corinthians 4:5).

We have also been charged with the privilege of showing what God is like and introducing people to Jesus Christ. The people who need you may be right there in your neighborhood, school, or workplace. Ask God for openings and creative approaches that your peers will respond to.

?

What are ways you could use your skills, gifts, and dreams
to serve others, both here and around the world?

³⁵ Then James and John, the sons of Zebedee, came to him. "Teacher," they said, "we want you to do for us whatever we ask."

³⁶ "What do you want me to do for you?" he asked.

³⁷ They replied, "Let one of us sit at your right and the other at your left in your glory."

³⁸ "You don't know what you are asking," Jesus said. "Can you drink the cup I drink or be baptized with the baptism I am baptized with?"

³⁹ "We can," they answered.

Jesus said to them, "You will drink the cup I drink and be baptized with the baptism I am baptized with, ⁴⁰ but to sit at my right or left is not for me to grant. These places belong to those for whom they have been prepared."

⁴¹ When the ten heard about this, they became indignant with James and John. ⁴² Jesus called them together and said, "You know that those who are regarded as rulers of the Gentiles lord it over them, and their high officials exercise authority over them. ⁴³ Not so with you. Instead, whoever wants to become great among you must be your servant, ⁴⁴ and whoever wants to be first must be slave of all. ⁴⁵ For even the Son of Man did not come to be served, but to serve, and to give his life as a ransom for many."

CREATING YOUR LIFE

Have you ever read a self-help book? The advice found in self-help books often sounds good—but the advice may be harder to follow. For example, one self-help author said this: do only what you're great at because that's when you'll be satisfied. The author was trying to help readers create the kind of life they wanted. But if we did only what we were great at, we probably wouldn't do much!

In Mark 10 we read about two disciples, James and John, who had plans for the kind of life they wanted for themselves someday. They asked to be at Jesus's right and left hand in His kingdom (v. 37). They were concerned with their reputations. They wanted to have influence.

Jesus then teaches them a different way of living—one of serving others. He said, "Whoever wants to become great among you must be your servant, and whoever wants to be first must be slave of all" (vv. 43–44). What is it about serving that makes us happy? After we save money to dig a well or build an orphanage, we feel better about ourselves, others, and God. Why is that?

Little chances to serve God and people happen all around us each day. Add to this list:

- "I'm heading to the kitchen for a glass of milk. Do you need anything while I'm there?"
- "Can I help you set up for your next class?"
- "How can pray for you?"
- "Since you forgot your lunch, do you want half of my sandwich?"

Even Jesus, the Son of God, "did not come to be served, but to serve" (v. 45). As we look at Christ's example and depend on the Holy Spirit's help, we too can be servants and live a purpose-filled life.

?

Who do you know that goes out of their way to serve others, and what impresses you about them?

[27] "But to you who are listening I [Jesus] say: Love your enemies, do good to those who hate you, [28] bless those who curse you, pray for those who mistreat you. [29] If someone slaps you on one cheek, turn to them the other also. If someone takes your coat, do not withhold your shirt from them. [30] Give to everyone who asks you, and if anyone takes what belongs to you, do not demand it back. [31] Do to others as you would have them do to you.

[32] "If you love those who love you, what credit is that to you? Even sinners love those who love them. [33] And if you do good to those who are good to you, what credit is that to you? Even sinners do that. [34] And if you lend to those from whom you expect repayment, what credit is that to you? Even sinners lend to sinners, expecting to be repaid in full. [35] But love your enemies, do good to them, and lend to them without expecting to get anything back. Then your reward will be great, and you will be children of the Most High, because he is kind to the ungrateful and wicked. [36] Be merciful, just as your Father is merciful.

STOP. THE. EVIL.

Thousands of people attend book festivals each year. Through them, you often get the chance to meet famous authors and get advice from professional writers. At one book festival, an author of young adult fiction told would-be writers, "Write the book that you want to find on the shelf." That's a powerful suggestion for writing and for living. What if we decided to live the way we want everyone else to live?

In Luke 6:27–36, Jesus calls His followers to seek a radical, courageous lifestyle—a lifestyle that works better than revenge. Better than, if you hate me, I'll hate you. Better than, if you slap me, I'll slap you harder. This passage calls for supernatural self-control. This stop-evil-in-its-tracks self-control comes from God's own Spirit (Galatians 5:22–23). We stop the path of evil rather than perpetuate it.

Not easy!

What does this look like in our everyday lives? What do you do, for example, when classmates hurl insults at the person sitting next to you at school? Or your sports team hazes some of your teammates? The passage teaches, "Do to others as you would have them do to you" (Luke 6:31), and that includes courageously speaking up for others.

Work to stop evil, not to continue it. Stop the natural pattern of you-started-it-so-I'll-get-you-worse retaliation. Stop. The. Evil. And let God's power show you how as you "pray for those who mistreat you" (v. 28).

Impossible? Yes, if we trust in our own strength. The strength instead comes from the Spirit—and from remembering how God has treated us. That's a life we all long to have.

?

Is there a culture of biting remarks or bullying in your home, at your school, or in your youth group? If so, what are ways you can start to stop the cycle?

¹⁶ Then the eleven disciples went to Galilee, to the mountain where Jesus had told them to go. ¹⁷ When they saw him, they worshiped him; but some doubted. ¹⁸ Then Jesus came to them and said, "All authority in heaven and on earth has been given to me. ¹⁹ Therefore go and make disciples of all nations, baptizing them in the name of the Father and of the Son and of the Holy Spirit, ²⁰ and teaching them to obey everything I have commanded you. And surely I am with you always, to the very end of the age."

ON THE DREAM TEAM

Who's on your dream team? Whether you participate in team chess, soccer, football, robotics, rugby, basketball, cheer, science olympiad, or any other activity, you can probably list the people you'd pick to play on your team! Jesus also picked stars but with very unexpected qualifications. He handpicked twelve men to follow and learn from Him. And then, after He died and came back to life, He gave those men the task of continuing His rescue mission. Who were these people He chose? Popular leaders? Superheroes? Nope. They were ordinary men—including working-class fishermen (Matthew 4:18–22) and a hated-because-he-cheated tax collector (Mark 2:14).

Jesus told them: "Go and make disciples of all nations" (Matthew 28:19). Regular people are stars because, well, they're regular! These people turned the world upside down, sharing the good news of Jesus Christ and leading uncounted numbers back to God.

These people worked in their groups of friends and acquaintances and with Jesus's authority. Jesus said: "All authority in heaven and on earth has been given to me" (v. 18). Jesus's dream team isn't about the players; it's about Him, our "team manager." We may not feel like much, but Jesus, the one with "all authority," is with us as we share His rescue with those we know. As you show your friends what Jesus is like, remember you're on His dream team!

———————— ? ————————

Talk with God about His purpose and assignments for you as part of His team.

[17] Unlike so many, we [Paul and others] do not peddle the word of God for profit. On the contrary, in Christ we speak before God with sincerity, as those sent from God.

3 [1] Are we beginning to commend ourselves again? Or do we need, like some people, letters of recommendation to you or from you? [2] You yourselves are our letter, written on our hearts, known and read by everyone. [3] You show that you are a letter from Christ, the result of our ministry, written not with ink but with the Spirit of the living God, not on tablets of stone but on tablets of human hearts.

PERMANENT

While in high school, a student wrote an essay about how much money was being spent on an athletic field in her local area—and how that money could have been spent to help more people in the community. Her teacher liked it and told her to send it to the local newspaper. The newspaper printed it as a guest column! Her simple essay reached more people than she had dreamed.

Whether it's writing, painting, acting, science, brain sports, athletics, or anything else, many of us want to do something that will put our names in the history books—something that will remind the world that we were here. But we don't have to wait until the books are written.

The history we're creating begins now.

What history are you writing into your friends' lives? Will they remember you as someone who is authentic? Persistent? Kind to everyone? Our actions may not get written down, but they will be remembered.

When Paul wrote letters on specific issues to local churches, he probably had no idea his words would still be read two thousand years later. Yet God still uses those letters as part of the New Testament to encourage and instruct us today. Even if God hadn't used Paul to write those letters, Paul's work would still have had unending value. "You yourselves are our letter," he wrote to the Corinthian Christians, "written on our hearts, known and read by everyone" (2 Corinthians 3:2). The people—not what gets printed—are what matter most. If you are a Christian, *you* are a letter from Christ to others.

So be encouraged! As you live for Jesus and look out for His people, anything you do will make a difference that will last. You are never forgotten by people, or by God.

Little things make a big difference—receiving a smile or a sneer, being included or being ignored, someone looking into your eyes or looking past you. What kind of difference do you want to make?

ROMANS 16:1-7

[1] I [Paul] commend to you our sister Phoebe, a deacon of the church in Cenchreae. [2] I ask you to receive her in the Lord in a way worthy of his people and to give her any help she may need from you, for she has been the benefactor of many people, including me.

[3] Greet Priscilla and Aquila, my co-workers in Christ Jesus. [4] They risked their lives for me. Not only I but all the churches of the Gentiles are grateful to them.

[5] Greet also the church that meets at their house.

Greet my dear friend Epenetus, who was the first convert to Christ in the province of Asia.

[6] Greet Mary, who worked very hard for you.

[7] Greet Andronicus and Junia, my fellow Jews who have been in prison with me. They are outstanding among the apostles, and they were in Christ before I was.

1 CORINTHIANS 15:58

Therefore, my dear brothers and sisters, stand firm. Let nothing move you. Always give yourselves fully to the work of the Lord, because you know that your labor in the Lord is not in vain.

RESCUE

On September 7, 1838, Grace Darling, the 22-year-old daughter of an English lighthouse keeper, spotted a shipwreck and survivors offshore. Twice, she and her father courageously rowed their boat a mile through stormy waters to rescue several people. Risking her life to rescue others, Grace became famous for her compassionate heart.

The apostle Paul tells us of another woman and man who took risks to rescue others. Priscilla and Aquila were a wife and husband team who worked as tentmakers alongside Paul while they found ways to teach people about Jesus. One action Priscilla and Aquila took was to explain the way of God more adequately to a Bible student and debater named Apollos. Priscilla and Aquila also "risked their lives for me" Paul wrote. "Not only I but all the churches of the Gentiles are grateful to them" (Romans 16:3–4).

The Bible doesn't specify the risk Paul referenced, but with beatings, imprisonment, shipwrecks, and death threats so common to Paul's ministry, it's not hard to see how this couple could have put themselves in harm's way to help their friend.

Rescuing others—whether from physical, emotional, relational, or spiritual danger—often carries a risk. Talk with God, so He can show you just what risks to take and how to handle each one.

If your name was in history books two hundred years from now, what action—perhaps one you haven't taken yet—would you want people to remember you for?

²⁵ But I [Paul] think it is necessary to send back to you Epaphroditus, my brother, co-worker and fellow soldier, who is also your messenger, whom you sent to take care of my needs. ²⁶ For he longs for all of you and is distressed because you heard he was ill. ²⁷ Indeed he was ill, and almost died. But God had mercy on him, and not on him only but also on me, to spare me sorrow upon sorrow. ²⁸ Therefore I am all the more eager to send him, so that when you see him again you may be glad and I may have less anxiety. ²⁹ So then, welcome him in the Lord with great joy, and honor people like him, ³⁰ because he almost died for the work of Christ. He risked his life to make up for the help you yourselves could not give me.

1 CORINTHIANS 15:58

Therefore, my dear brothers and sisters, stand firm. Let nothing move you. Always give yourselves fully to the work of the Lord, because you know that your labor in the Lord is not in vain.

AT RISK FOR JESUS

During basic military training, Desmond Doss annoyed his instructor and the other soldiers. As a pacifist—someone who is against violence and war, also called a conscientious objector—he refused to carry a weapon into battle, which made onlookers think he was afraid. Trained as a medic, this young Christian went into a war zone to save lives.

When his military unit faced the enemy, the other soldiers began to change their minds about Desmond. During one World War II battle, he ducked under machine gun fire to pull the wounded to safety. He prayed, "Lord, give me the strength to save just one more wounded soldier." Eventually he lowered more than seventy injured men down a hill for further medical attention. For his efforts he was awarded the highest military honor.

The Bible tells us about another Christian who took great risks to help others, Epaphroditus. Paul wrote this about him: "Welcome him in the Lord with great joy, and honor people like him, because he almost died for the work of Christ" (Philippians 2:29–30).

Your risks may be similar or different. You may risk your reputation or image, a relationship, even some sleep. But when God leads you to take a particular risk, He will give you the power to master it. You and others around the world today matter to the cause of Christ.

?

What risk might you courageously undertake? If it doesn't contradict what the Bible teaches and can glorify God, that's the kind of risk worth taking!

1 CORINTHIANS 4:10-17

¹⁰ We [Paul and others] are fools for Christ, but you are so wise in Christ! We are weak, but you are strong! You are honored, we are dishonored! ¹¹ To this very hour we go hungry and thirsty, we are in rags, we are brutally treated, we are homeless. ¹² We work hard with our own hands. When we are cursed, we bless; when we are persecuted, we endure it; ¹³ when we are slandered, we answer kindly. We have become the scum of the earth, the garbage of the world—right up to this moment.

¹⁴ I am writing this not to shame you but to warn you as my dear children. ¹⁵ Even if you had ten thousand guardians in Christ, you do not have many fathers, for in Christ Jesus I became your father through the gospel. ¹⁶ Therefore I urge you to imitate me. ¹⁷ For this reason I have sent to you Timothy, my son whom I love, who is faithful in the Lord. He will remind you of my way of life in Christ Jesus, which agrees with what I teach everywhere in every church.

COURAGE TO BE ME

An ad for watches promoted its brightly colored wristbands. The ad said you could make sure the watch wristband never matches your clothes; that way people will notice your watch because of its different color: "They'll see that you have 'color courage.' And they'll want to be like you." Whatever your thoughts on those watches, the ad has a point: most of us do like to be noticed!

If you do a quick reading of 1 Corinthians 4, you might think Paul sounds a bit full of himself when he says we should follow his example (v. 16). But looking closer at 1 Corinthians, we see why he wrote so confidently. He could ask people to be like him because he copied Jesus, the greatest Servant of all. "Follow my example, as I follow the example of Christ" (11:1). Paul only wanted others to look at him because he knew they would then see something of Jesus.

If we want people to like us for the right reasons and to be like us in the right ways, we must first be like Jesus. Then, even when we don't say it out loud, we can bravely live in a way that urges others to imitate what we say and do. If we have any reason for people to follow our example—if we have the courage to point others to the Savior—it is because of Him, not us.

?

Paul, following Jesus, became courageous. What is one way you—as a follower of Jesus—can live fearlessly this week?

1 KINGS 14:7-11, 14-16

⁷ Go, tell Jeroboam that this is what the LORD, the God of Israel, says: "I raised you up from among the people and appointed you ruler over my people Israel. ⁸ I tore the kingdom away from the house of David and gave it to you, but you have not been like my servant David, who kept my commands and followed me with all his heart, doing only what was right in my eyes. ⁹ You have done more evil than all who lived before you. You have made for yourself other gods, idols made of metal; you have aroused my anger and turned your back on me.

¹⁰ "'Because of this, I am going to bring disaster on the house of Jeroboam. I will cut off from Jeroboam every last male in Israel—slave or free. I will burn up the house of Jeroboam as one burns dung, until it is all gone. ¹¹ Dogs will eat those belonging to Jeroboam who die in the city, and the birds will feed on those who die in the country. The LORD has spoken!" . . .

¹⁴ The LORD will raise up for himself a king over Israel who will cut off the family of Jeroboam. Even now this is beginning to happen. ¹⁵ And the LORD will strike Israel, so that it will be like a reed swaying in the water. He will uproot Israel from this good land that he gave to their ancestors and scatter them beyond the Euphrates River, because they aroused the Lord's anger by making Asherah poles. ¹⁶ And he will give Israel up because of the sins Jeroboam has committed and has caused Israel to commit.

BAD, MOSTLY BAD, EXTRA BAD

God warned against His people having a king. Why? If you read about the kings of the Old Testament, you'll see one reason why.

Only a few of the kings are labeled "good" in the Old Testament. Most of them are "bad," "mostly bad," "extra bad," or "the worst."

We can choose to be a good influence or a bad influence. King David was described as a good king who "followed [God] with all his heart" (1 Kings 14:8). He's held up as a good example to follow (3:14; 11:38).

The bad kings rejected God. They led the people to follow other "gods" and do their own thing. King Jeroboam is remembered as one of the worst of these kings—"who sinned and who made Israel sin" (14:16 NKJV). God's message to him was: "You have done more evil than all who lived before you" (14:9).

It may sound almost exciting to do more evil than anyone else has done. But you would make yourself, as well as dozens of others, miserable. Because of Jeroboam's bad influence, many kings who came after him followed in his footsteps and are described as being as evil as he was (16:2, 19, 26, 31; 22:52).

It may be hard for you to believe, but you do have influence, whether in a formal leadership position or not. You choose which type of influence you will be. People around will be affected whichever way you go.

—— ? ——

How can use your influence—through your involvement at church, school, work, even at home—for good? Talk with Jesus about it to hear His ideas.

16 How much better to get wisdom than gold,
   to get insight rather than silver!

17 The highway of the upright avoids evil;
   those who guard their ways preserve their lives.

18 Pride goes before destruction,
   a haughty spirit before a fall.

19 Better to be lowly in spirit along with the oppressed
   than to share plunder with the proud.

20 Whoever gives heed to instruction prospers,
   and blessed is the one who trusts in the Lord.

21 The wise in heart are called discerning,
   and gracious words promote instruction.

22 Prudence is a fountain of life to the prudent,
   but folly brings punishment to fools.

NOTHING TO PROVE

People who do great things and become famous during their lifetimes are sometimes called "legends in their own time." A man who played soccer at the international level says he has met many people in the world of sport who were only "legends in their own mind." Our pride has a way of puffing up how we see ourselves, and we start thinking we're the best thing ever! But humility means we see ourselves as we really are—as God sees us—with all our strengths *and* weaknesses.

Another danger with wrongful pride is that we assume the rules don't apply to us—that we are an exception for some reason. The writer of Proverbs said, "Pride goes before destruction, a haughty spirit before a fall" (16:18). Seeing ourselves as better than we really are, or at least better than everyone else, can lead us to bigger problems as it makes us more distant with friends.

The answer to our pride is the humility that comes from knowing God. "Better to be lowly in spirit along with the oppressed than to share plunder with the proud" (v. 19). Jesus explained, "Whoever wants to become great among you must be your servant, and whoever wants to be first must be your slave—just as the Son of Man did not come to be served, but to serve, and to give his life as a ransom for many" (Matthew 20:26–28).

There is nothing wrong with enjoying success while using the skills God gives us in useful activities—God celebrates with us. The challenge is to stay focused on Jesus and his purposes rather than drawing attention to ourselves. When we're secure in Jesus, we don't have to prove anything to anybody.

When is pride godly and when is pride destructive? How do they look different to others?

PHILIPPIANS 2:3-8

³ Do nothing out of selfish ambition or vain conceit. Rather, in humility value others above yourselves, ⁴ not looking to your own interests but each of you to the interests of the others.

⁵ In your relationships with one another, have the same mindset as Christ Jesus:

⁶ Who, being in very nature God,
  did not consider equality with God something to be
    used to his own advantage;
⁷ rather, he made himself nothing
  by taking the very nature of a servant,
  being made in human likeness.
⁸ And being found in appearance as a man,
  he humbled himself
  by becoming obedient to death—
    even death on a cross!

AMBITION

Lacks drive and ambition." That is *not* something you want written to a potential employer in a recommendation letter from a teacher. You definitely don't want it written on your end-of-semester report at school either. It would not be a great thing for your parents to read about your school experience.

We need to have some drive in our lives. Otherwise we'd never get out of bed, never bother eating, never go to school, never gain the knowledge and strengthen the skills we need to accomplish our dreams, never grow the type of love that makes a marriage work. But drive and ambition have a dark side we should be aware of. It can easily become "selfish ambition" (Philippians 2:3), which is all about doing things to make our own lives better at any cost—even if others get stomped on along the way.

This was the case with many of the kings of Israel, including the first one. Saul started out with humility, but he became rather full of himself. He thought of his role of king as something that belonged to him. He forgot that his role was to lead God's people in ways that would show them, and the other nations around them, the way to God. When God decided to take the role of king away from him, Saul's only thoughts were for himself: "I have sinned. But . . ." (1 Samuel 15:30).

In a world where ambition often means pushing others out of the way to get what we want, we have the freedom to live differently. We do nothing out of "selfish ambition" and put away anything that makes us live in that way (Hebrews 12:1). Instead, we choose real ambition, the God-centered kind that does the right thing on the way to accomplishing great things.

Selfish ambition or God-centered ambition—what proportion of each did you display yesterday? What proportion of each do you want to display tomorrow?

EPHESIANS 3:8-19

[8] Although I [Paul] am less than the least of all the Lord's people, this grace was given me: to preach to the Gentiles the boundless riches of Christ, [9] and to make plain to everyone the administration of this mystery, which for ages past was kept hidden in God, who created all things. [10] His intent was that now, through the church, the manifold wisdom of God should be made known to the rulers and authorities in the heavenly realms, [11] according to his eternal purpose that he accomplished in Christ Jesus our Lord. [12] In him and through faith in him we may approach God with freedom and confidence. [13] I ask you, therefore, not to be discouraged because of my sufferings for you, which are your glory.

[14] For this reason I kneel before the Father, [15] from whom every family in heaven and on earth derives its name. [16] I pray that out of his glorious riches he may strengthen you with power through his Spirit in your inner being, [17] so that Christ may dwell in your hearts through faith. And I pray that you, being rooted and established in love, [18] may have power, together with all the Lord's holy people, to grasp how wide and long and high and deep is the love of Christ, [19] and to know this love that surpasses knowledge—that you may be filled to the measure of all the fullness of God.

PERFECTLY IMPERFECT

Advice from a teacher to one of his students: Stop trying to write perfect essays. The student was taking so much time to make her work perfect, she never really finished. In fact, she often gave up halfway through because it was so hard. The teacher suggested that if she accepted that her work would never be totally perfect, she would be able to write more freely and grow more in what she did.

Paul gave an even better reason to stop trying to be perfect: Jesus has already made us so. Yes, we have some growing to do, but we have a solid foundation on which to build.

Paul had learned this the hard way. After years of trying to perfectly follow what he thought he was supposed to do—and all that time actually *disobeying* God—Jesus corrected his wayward path (Galatians 1:11–16).

This doesn't mean we shouldn't be bothered when we get things wrong or that we should just wait for Jesus to fix things, but it does mean we should let ourselves be "rooted and established" in God's love (Ephesians 3:17). We can focus on doing rightly rather than doing perfectly.

In this lifetime, we will always be works in progress. But as we continue to depend on Jesus, He will work in us (v. 16). In Him we are free to grow ever deeper in the love "too great" to ever "understand fully" (v. 19 NLT).

?

Why do you want to improve? Talk with God about those reasons and what He'd like you to do first.

⁸ Then the man and his wife heard the sound of the LORD God as he was walking in the garden in the cool of the day, and they hid from the LORD GOD among the trees of the garden. ⁹ But the LORD God called to the man, "Where are you?"

¹⁰ He answered, "I heard you in the garden, and I was afraid because I was naked; so I hid."

¹¹ And he said, "Who told you that you were naked? Have you eaten from the tree that I commanded you not to eat from?"

¹² The man said, "The woman you put here with me—she gave me some fruit from the tree, and I ate it."

¹³ Then the LORD God said to the woman, "What is this you have done?"

The woman said, "The serpent deceived me, and I ate."

Read the whole passage: Genesis 3:1–13.

BLAME GAME

It's easy to blame other people. We might even *believe* they are actually responsible for what we've done or failed to do. "I wouldn't have gone there if so-and-so hadn't told me about it . . ." or "I *said* it was a bad idea, but nobody listened."

Blaming others has been around since the very first people messed up. When Adam and Eve ate from the one tree God had told them to leave alone, their eyes were opened and they lost their happiness. God asked two questions: "Where are you?" (Genesis 3:9) and "Have you eaten from the tree that I commanded you not to eat from?" (v. 11). Then the blame game started:

"The woman you put here with me—she gave me some fruit from the tree, and I ate it" (v. 12). Adam blamed both the woman and God for his sin. Blaming God? That's bold and foolish! Then Eve blamed the serpent. Do you think she really was deceived? Or did she know and just want the fruit?

Ever since that day in the garden of Eden, and even as toddlers, we tend to blame others for our choices. But it is pretty rare when someone else is actually responsible for our actions.

When we mess up—even if we do so unknowingly—we should own up. The first step in saying "I'm sorry" is to admit we did something wrong. "What now, God?" comes next. Only then can we find forgiveness and get back on the path to living joyfully.

$$?$$

What do you tend to blame for your sinful actions—a bad mood, too much pressure, tiredness, a person? Decide that you're going to accept responsibility for your sin today!

ACTS 7:59–8:8

⁵⁹ While they were stoning him, Stephen prayed, "Lord Jesus, receive my spirit." ⁶⁰ Then he fell on his knees and cried out, "Lord, do not hold this sin against them." When he had said this, he fell asleep.

8 ¹ And Saul approved of their killing him.

On that day a great persecution broke out against the church in Jerusalem, and all except the apostles were scattered throughout Judea and Samaria. ² Godly men buried Stephen and mourned deeply for him. ³ But Saul began to destroy the church. Going from house to house, he dragged off both men and women and put them in prison.

⁴ Those who had been scattered preached the word wherever they went. ⁵ Philip went down to a city in Samaria and proclaimed the Messiah there. ⁶ When the crowds heard Philip and saw the signs he performed, they all paid close attention to what he said. ⁷ For with shrieks, impure spirits came out of many, and many who were paralyzed or lame were healed. ⁸ So there was great joy in that city.

THE VIRAL GOSPEL

If you're like most teenagers, you've watched your share of viral videos. These videos may be funny, inspiring, thought-provoking, or a combination of all three. Having a post go viral is an advertiser's dream, but few marketing experts are able to exploit it. Marketing expert Lacy Kemp wrote, "How do you make something spread like wildfire? The answer is that you can't. It's not something to plan for or else everyone would be doing it. It has to be awesome enough on its own to get there."

That's the way it is with the gospel of Jesus Christ—it's awesome enough on its own to get there. It spreads from one person to another.

It's been spreading since before the internet and will keep spreading no matter what technology comes next.

Why? Because the God of the universe has come personally to individuals. God loves us and shows it. Stephen, a leader in the early church, was stoned to death (literally, people threw stones at him until he died). As a result, followers of Jesus in Jerusalem were forced to leave their homes (Acts 8:1–3). Instead of fearfully holding back, these Christians told people about Jesus wherever they moved, and the gospel became viral. "Those who had been scattered preached the word wherever they went" (v. 4).

You are continuing this contagiousness of the gospel. You can share it with your words, but sometimes even more with your actions. When you show care, people want to know why. They may watch you for years to see whether what you believe about God is true. It is!

What is something you can share about God in the next couple days?

[1] The LORD said to Moses, [2] "Speak to the entire assembly of Israel and say to them: 'Be holy because I, the LORD your God, am holy.

[3] "'Each of you must respect your mother and father, and you must observe my Sabbaths. I am the LORD your God.

[4] "'Do not turn to idols or make metal gods for yourselves. I am the LORD your God. . . .

[33] "'When a foreigner resides among you in your land, do not mistreat them. [34] The foreigner residing among you must be treated as your native-born. Love them as yourself, for you were foreigners in Egypt. I am the LORD your God.

[35] "'Do not use dishonest standards when measuring length, weight or quantity. [36] Use honest scales and honest weights, an honest ephah [a dry measure] and an honest hin [a liquid measure]. I am the LORD your God, who brought you out of Egypt.

[37] "'Keep all my decrees and all my laws and follow them. I am the LORD.'"

STRANGERS WELCOMING STRANGERS

A family moved to another country, and they didn't know where they would live or work for a time. A local church helped them find a rental house with many bedrooms. They lived in two bedrooms and rented the others to international students. The family and their housemates then welcomed dozens of others into the home every Friday night for a Bible study. For three years, the family members were strangers welcoming strangers: sharing their home and meals with people from all over the world.

During a time in their history, God's people knew what it meant to be far from home. For several hundred years, the Israelites were foreigners—and slaves—in Egypt.

The Bible describes us as "foreigners" on earth (1 Peter 2:11). We may struggle to find a friend to sit with at lunch. We yearn for belonging in a group of people who truly understand us. We don't feel like we fit in. And we're not supposed to!

God gets that and shows us what to do in the book of Leviticus. In Leviticus 19, alongside instructions like "respect your mother and father" and "do not steal" (vv. 3, 11), God reminded His people to care: "When a foreigner resides among you in your land, do not mistreat them. . . . Love them as yourself, for you were foreigners in Egypt. . . . I am the LORD your God, who brought you out of Egypt. Keep all my decrees" (Leviticus 19:33–37).

We strangers are to welcome other strangers.

Who can you look out for today? Why are all people more alike than different?

ACTS 6:1-7

¹ In those days when the number of disciples was increasing, the Hellenistic Jews among them complained against the Hebraic Jews because their widows were being overlooked in the daily distribution of food. ² So the Twelve gathered all the disciples together and said, "It would not be right for us to neglect the ministry of the word of God in order to wait on tables. ³ Brothers and sisters, choose seven men from among you who are known to be full of the Spirit and wisdom. We will turn this responsibility over to them ⁴ and will give our attention to prayer and the ministry of the word."

⁵ This proposal pleased the whole group. They chose Stephen, a man full of faith and of the Holy Spirit; also Philip, Procorus, Nicanor, Timon, Parmenas, and Nicolas from Antioch, a convert to Judaism. ⁶ They presented these men to the apostles, who prayed and laid their hands on them.

⁷ So the word of God spread. The number of disciples in Jerusalem increased rapidly, and a large number of priests became obedient to the faith.

SOLVE IT

Some towns grow fast. Maybe Amazon moves into town and there are suddenly three thousand new jobs. People move into the area. Some speak different languages. All will have different customs, even if they're just from a different part of your own country.

Growth challenges aren't new to the church (see Acts 6:1). When new people come into the church, it can make for awkward situations and noticeable difficulties. Longtime churchgoers need to welcome newcomers. And newcomers need to welcome the old. We're all in this God-serving business together.

Misunderstandings and arguments can happen. Some say where there are two Christians, there will be three opinions! If we don't deal with the problems in the right way, bigger problems will grow.

Here's an example from the early Christian church in Jerusalem. The Greek-speaking Jews (the Hellenists) had a problem with the Jews who spoke Aramaic. They believed the Hellenist widows "were being overlooked in the daily distribution of food" (Acts 6:1). So the apostles told the church to "choose seven men from among you who are known to be full of the Spirit and wisdom" (v. 3). The seven men chosen all had Greek names (v. 5). These first deacons would have been Hellenists, members of the group with the problem. The apostles prayed over them, and the church kept on growing (vv. 6–7).

Adding new people in a school classroom or in a youth group setting can be a bit scary. We might be tempted to just ignore them, especially if there is more than one new person, and just let them hang out together. But as we ask the Holy Spirit to help us, we'll find ways to support one another and learn from one another. We'll show the world that we are united by our loving God, and word about Him will spread.

?

Where do you need to be a force for unity? Pray for the Holy Spirit's guidance.

DAY 54

[30] The apostles gathered around Jesus and reported to him all they had done and taught. [31] Then, because so many people were coming and going that they did not even have a chance to eat, he said to them, "Come with me by yourselves to a quiet place and get some rest."

[32] So they went away by themselves in a boat to a solitary place. [33] But many who saw them leaving recognized them and ran on foot from all the towns and got there ahead of them. [34] When Jesus landed and saw a large crowd, he had compassion on them, because they were like sheep without a shepherd. So he began teaching them many things.

[35] By this time it was late in the day, so his disciples came to him. "This is a remote place," they said, "and it's already very late. [36] Send the people away so that they can go to the surrounding countryside and villages and buy themselves something to eat."

[37] But he answered, "You give them something to eat."

DO IT YOURSELF

You give them something to eat" (Mark 6:37). It's easy to miss those words from Jesus. A huge crowd of five thousand men plus their families had gathered to hear Jesus. As the day got later, His friends started trying to get Him to send the crowd away to "buy themselves something to eat" (v. 36). "You give them something to eat," Jesus replied (v. 37).

Why would He say that? John 6:6 says He was testing them. It seems He wanted His friends to get involved in caring for the crowd, to be hands-on in working with and for Him.

As part of this process, Jesus directed the men to divide the people into groups of hundreds and fifties. Jesus then took what the disciples brought to Him—five loaves of bread and two fish—and fed everyone, with "twelve basketfuls" of leftovers (Mark 6:43).

I think Jesus uses words like these with us too. Maybe we see a friend who's struggling or a problem that needs fixing and we talk to God about it. "You do something," He says. He then shows us what to do and how to do it. You are trusted by God himself to be involved with His need-meeting work.

?

What's happening with the people around you?

⁴⁵ Immediately Jesus made his disciples get into the boat and go on ahead of him to Bethsaida, while he dismissed the crowd. ⁴⁶ After leaving them, he went up on a mountainside to pray.

⁴⁷ Later that night, the boat was in the middle of the lake, and he was alone on land. ⁴⁸ He saw the disciples straining at the oars, because the wind was against them. Shortly before dawn he went out to them, walking on the lake. He was about to pass by them, ⁴⁹ but when they saw him walking on the lake, they thought he was a ghost. They cried out, ⁵⁰ because they all saw him and were terrified.

Immediately he spoke to them and said, "Take courage! It is I. Don't be afraid." ⁵¹ Then he climbed into the boat with them, and the wind died down. They were completely amazed, ⁵² for they had not understood about the loaves; their hearts were hardened.

⁵³ When they had crossed over, they landed at Gennesaret and anchored there.

FEAR RELEASE

What do you do when you're scared? Does blood pump in your ears? Is there a weight in your stomach? Does your heart pound? Do you become breathless? Our bodies respond to fear like this so we can get ready to run from danger. It's called the fight-or-flight response.

Jesus's followers may have felt all these things one night after He had fed more than five thousand people with just one packed lunch. Jesus had sent them ahead to Bethsaida so He could be alone to pray. During the night, they were rowing against the wind when suddenly they saw Him walking on the water. Thinking He was a ghost, they were terrified (Mark 6:49–50).

But Jesus told them not to be afraid and to be brave. As He got on the boat, the wind died down, and they made it to the shore. Whew! Close one!

As Jesus answers our fears with His presence, we can know calm, even in the middle of storms, a peace that "exceeds anything we can understand" (Philippians 4:7 NLT). We can also do whatever Jesus tells us to do next.

?

Some fears can be managed easily. Some are genuinely dangerous. Talk with God about both types in your life and what to do about each.

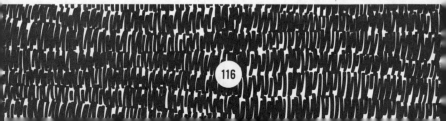

GENESIS 41:53-57

⁵³ The seven years of abundance in Egypt came to an end, ⁵⁴ and the seven years of famine began, just as Joseph had said. There was famine in all the other lands, but in the whole land of Egypt there was food. ⁵⁵ When all Egypt began to feel the famine, the people cried to Pharaoh for food. Then Pharaoh told all the Egyptians, "Go to Joseph and do what he tells you."

⁵⁶ When the famine had spread over the whole country, Joseph opened all the storehouses and sold grain to the Egyptians, for the famine was severe throughout Egypt. ⁵⁷ And all the world came to Egypt to buy grain from Joseph, because the famine was severe everywhere.

Read the whole passage: Genesis 41:46–57.

HEBREWS 13:15-16

¹⁵ Through Jesus, therefore, let us continually offer to God a sacrifice of praise—the fruit of lips that openly profess his name. ¹⁶ And do not forget to do good and to share with others, for with such sacrifices God is pleased.

YOU ARE CRITICAL TO THE PROCESS

After a terrible accident at a school during which some students lost their lives, people wanted to help in whatever way they could. Some donated blood for the injured; some gave free food and drinks for the rescue workers. Other people sent gifts of money and teddy bears for the survivors. Many offered to just sit with the shocked teachers and students.

You can use your gifts to help others too. A man in the Bible showed a bit of how to help: (1) he looked ahead, (2) he listened to God, (3) he made a plan, (4) he got people involved. This man's name was Joseph, and he helped Egypt through a seven-year food shortage. His help meant everyone managed to have enough to eat (Genesis 41:53–54). When Joseph told Pharaoh, the king of Egypt, that hard years were coming, Pharaoh put Joseph in charge of getting the country ready. God had given Joseph the skills and abilities to prepare (v. 39). Then, "when the famine had spread over the whole country, Joseph opened all the store-houses" (v. 56). He was even able to help his own family (45:16–18).

God has given you skills and abilities. When you see people in need—whether here or around the world—be willing to help. Around the world, people don't have clean water. You can raise money to help them drill a well. At your school, there are those who are lonely. You could sit with them at lunch or say hello to them in the hallway. What else might God guide you to do? Listen to God. He will show you.

?

What help or care can you show to someone today? Ask God for eyes to see where you are needed.

ROMANS 9:1–5 NLT

[1] With Christ as my witness, I [Paul] speak with utter truthfulness. My conscience and the Holy Spirit confirm it. [2] My heart is filled with bitter sorrow and unending grief [3] for my people, my Jewish brothers and sisters. I would be willing to be forever cursed—cut off from Christ!—if that would save them. [4] They are the people of Israel, chosen to be God's adopted children. God revealed his glory to them. He made covenants with them and gave them his law. He gave them the privilege of worshiping him and receiving his wonderful promises. [5] Abraham, Isaac, and Jacob are their ancestors, and Christ himself was an Israelite as far as his human nature is concerned. And he is God, the one who rules over everything and is worthy of eternal praise! Amen

A LOVE TO SHARE

After becoming a Christian and until his death at age thirty-four, Nabeel Qureshi wrote books and spoke around the world to help other Christians understand the people in the religion he left behind. He lectured at over one hundred universities. He earned four postgraduate degrees. He was a Christian apologist, which means he showed evidence for God's reality and the Bible's reliability. Qureshi dedicated one of his books to his sister, who had not yet trusted in Jesus. The dedication is short but powerful: "I am begging God for the day that we can worship Him together." Through it all, Qureshi showed love for the people of his former religion.

We get a sense of that same deep love for people as we read Paul's letter to the church in Rome. "My heart is filled with bitter sorrow and unending grief," he said, "for my people, my Jewish brothers and sisters. I would be willing to be forever cursed—cut off from Christ!—if that would save them" (Romans 9:2–3 NLT).

Paul loved the Jewish people so much that he would have chosen to be cut off from God himself if only they would accept Jesus. He understood that by rejecting Jesus, his people were rejecting the one true God. This made him urge his readers to share the good news of Jesus with everyone (10:14–15).

Many Christians choose an unreached people group to pray for and to pour energy into. Investigate groups who may never have had an opportunity to learn about Jesus—in your own school or around the globe. Talk with God about one of those groups regularly, asking how you might help to reach them.

?

What people group tugs on your heart? Maybe a group at your school? Maybe someone you have something in common with?

¹³ Brothers and sisters, we [Paul and others] do not want you to be uninformed about those who sleep in death, so that you do not grieve like the rest of mankind, who have no hope. ¹⁴ For we believe that Jesus died and rose again, and so we believe that God will bring with Jesus those who have fallen asleep in him. ¹⁵ According to the Lord's word, we tell you that we who are still alive, who are left until the coming of the Lord, will certainly not precede those who have fallen asleep. ¹⁶ For the Lord himself will come down from heaven, with a loud command, with the voice of the archangel and with the trumpet call of God, and the dead in Christ will rise first. ¹⁷ After that, we who are still alive and are left will be caught up together with them in the clouds to meet the Lord in the air. And so we will be with the Lord forever. ¹⁸ Therefore encourage one another with these words.

ALWAYS

What do you think of the words *always* and *never*? They can hold so much hope! We could think that we could "always" be happy and that life would "never" fail us. However, reality says that we won't always be happy and that the things we hope would never happen just might happen. So, as good as these wishes sound, they struggle to live up to their potential—unless we're thinking about the promise of Jesus's presence.

To a group of troubled disciples who feared the challenges ahead, Jesus said, "I am with you always" (Matthew 28:20). The writer to the Hebrews reminds us that God said, "'I will never leave you nor forsake you.' So we may boldly say: 'The LORD is my helper, I will not fear'" (Hebrews 13:5–6 NKJV).

Think about this promise and what it means: "We shall always be with the Lord" (1 Thessalonians 4:17 NKJV). How encouraging! God walks next to you when you are frightened, or worried, or sick, or lonely. He's there when you knock that ball out of the park for a grand slam, and He's there when you strike out. He's there as you pick the person to date, and as you recognize the ones to avoid dating.

No matter how scary your journey is or how hopeless your future looks, God will go with you to give you courage and comfort to make it through.

What makes you wonder if God will leave you or has already left you? How do you know He is absolutely still there with you?

²⁸ "What do you think? There was a man who had two sons. He went to the first and said, 'Son, go and work today in the vineyard.'

²⁹ "'I will not,' he answered, but later he changed his mind and went.

³⁰ "Then the father went to the other son and said the same thing. He answered, 'I will, sir,' but he did not go.

³¹ "Which of the two did what his father wanted?"

"The first," they answered.

Jesus said to them, "Truly I tell you, the tax collectors and the prostitutes are entering the kingdom of God ahead of you. ³² For John came to you to show you the way of righteousness, and you did not believe him, but the tax collectors and the prostitutes did. And even after you saw this, you did not repent and believe him."

I DON'T FEEL LIKE IT

You know how it is—when someone tells you what to do, you tend to do the opposite, even if it's something you know you need to do. Homework. Clean your room. Chores. Plan your sports strategy. Go to lessons. Practice for those lessons. Take care of a sibling. You just can't be bothered!

Sometimes the stuff that needs doing is the last thing we want to do. When this situation arises, try repeating this motto: "I don't feel like it—but I'm going to do it anyway."

Jesus taught about this value of taking action. He told about two sons whose father instructed them to work in the vineyard. The first said no, but "later he changed his mind and went" (Matthew 21:29). The second said "I will, sir," but did nothing. This second boy was all talk and no action. He may have charmed his dad, but he didn't get the job done. Then Jesus asked His listeners, "Which of the two did what his father wanted?" (v. 31). The obvious answer: the one who finished the job.

Jesus then explained the meaning in verses 31–32. We can be in church and do all the churchy things and say all the churchy words but if we don't show real love and real action every day, we haven't pleased God, our Father. He's interested in action—the action that creates goodness for the people around us. God is interested in our faith and obedience—not just our good intentions.

Next time you can't be bothered to do something, it's okay to admit that to God. Go ahead and say, "I don't feel like it," and then ask Him for the strength to do it anyway.

What would your life look like if you did what God told you to do, even when you didn't feel like it?

ROMANS 8:22-26

²² We know that the whole creation has been groaning as in the pains of childbirth right up to the present time. ²³ Not only so, but we ourselves, who have the firstfruits of the Spirit, groan inwardly as we wait eagerly for our adoption to sonship, the redemption of our bodies. ²⁴ For in this hope we were saved. But hope that is seen is no hope at all. Who hopes for what they already have? ²⁵ But if we hope for what we do not yet have, we wait for it patiently.

²⁶ In the same way, the Spirit helps us in our weakness. We do not know what we ought to pray for, but the Spirit himself intercedes for us through wordless groans.

WHEN YOU JUST CAN'T PRAY

Josh needed surgery. Except for when he was born, he had never even been in a hospital before, let alone had an operation.

It was all he could think about. It felt big, maybe bigger than anything he'd had to deal with before.

He had so many questions. "Will I die?" he asked. "Are there people I need to make things right with first?" He wondered how long he would be in the hospital; what make-up work he'd need to do before and after; how long it would take before he could get back to life as normal; if life would *ever* get back to normal. It was a time both to get things done and to pray.

But he couldn't do either.

He was so weary and worried that even the simplest of tasks seemed impossible. He wanted to be strong and confident, but he had a lot of fears. When he tried to pray, his thoughts would wander, and he couldn't put two words together.

Thankfully, the Holy Spirit helps us in our weakness (Romans 8:26).

When Josh couldn't figure out what to say, God still knew what was in Josh's heart. After all, God had lived on Earth and had experienced all the normal feelings of life.

For those who understand and accept that Jesus Christ is the only way to God, when we can't pray or don't know what we should pray, the Spirit does it for us. How great is that!

?

When have you been at a total loss for words during prayer—whether because of nervousness, excitement, fear, or something else? How does it feel to know that there were still prayers for you in that moment?

LUKE 15:11-24

[11] Jesus continued: "There was a man who had two sons. [12] The younger one said to his father, 'Father, give me my share of the estate.' So he divided his property between them.

[13] "Not long after that, the younger son got together all he had, set off for a distant country and there squandered his wealth in wild living. [14] After he had spent everything, there was a severe famine in that whole country, and he began to be in need. [15] So he went and hired himself out to a citizen of that country, who sent him to his fields to feed pigs. [16] He longed to fill his stomach with the pods that the pigs were eating, but no one gave him anything.

[17] "When he came to his senses, he said, 'How many of my father's hired servants have food to spare, and here I am starving to death! [18] I will set out and go back to my father and say to him: Father, I have sinned against heaven and against you. [19] I am no longer worthy to be called your son; make me like one of your hired servants.' [20] So he got up and went to his father.

"But while he was still a long way off, his father saw him and was filled with compassion for him; he ran to his son, threw his arms around him and kissed him.

[21] "The son said to him, 'Father, I have sinned against heaven and against you. I am no longer worthy to be called your son.'

[22] "But the father said to his servants, 'Quick! Bring the best robe and put it on him. Put a ring on his finger and sandals on his feet. [23] Bring the fattened calf and kill it. Let's have a feast and celebrate. [24] For this son of mine was dead and is alive again; he was lost and is found.' So they began to celebrate."

THE RANCHER

During one summer vacation, David worked on a ranch for a few weeks. One evening, tired and hungry after a long day, he drove the tractor into the yard. Acting like a hotshot, he cranked the steering wheel hard left, stamped on the left brake, and spun the tractor around. The back of the tractor caught one of the legs holding up a 500-gallon gasoline tank. The tank hit the ground with a loud boom. Gasoline was everywhere.

The rancher stood nearby, watching.

David got off the tractor, stammered an apology, and—because it was the first thing that popped into his mind—offered to work the rest of the summer for free.

The farmer stared at the wreckage for a moment and turned toward the house. "Let's go have dinner," he said. A story Jesus told passed through David's mind—about a young man who had done some terrible things. The young man in the story told his dad: "Father, I have sinned against heaven and against you." He had planned to add, "Make me like one of your hired servants," but before he could get all the words out of his mouth, his dad stopped him (Luke 15:17–24). It was like he said, "Let's go have dinner."

Like that dad, David's boss was an incredible picture of God's amazing forgiveness and loving grace. "Oh, what joy for those whose disobedience is forgiven, whose sin is put out of sight!" (Psalm 32:1 NLT).

———————— ? ————————

Think over some foolish things you've done. Why did you choose to do them? Whose forgiveness did you need?

¹² Just as a body, though one, has many parts, but all its many parts form one body, so it is with Christ. ¹³ For we were all baptized by one Spirit so as to form one body—whether Jews or Gentiles, slave or free—and we were all given the one Spirit to drink. ¹⁴ Even so the body is not made up of one part but of many.

¹⁵ Now if the foot should say, "Because I am not a hand, I do not belong to the body," it would not for that reason stop being part of the body. ¹⁶ And if the ear should say, "Because I am not an eye, I do not belong to the body," it would not for that reason stop being part of the body. ¹⁷ If the whole body were an eye, where would the sense of hearing be? If the whole body were an ear, where would the sense of smell be? ¹⁸ But in fact God has placed the parts in the body, every one of them, just as he wanted them to be. ¹⁹ If they were all one part, where would the body be? ²⁰ As it is, there are many parts, but one body.

²¹ The eye cannot say to the hand, "I don't need you!" And the head cannot say to the feet, "I don't need you!" ²² On the contrary, those parts of the body that seem to be weaker are indispensable, ²³ and the parts that we think are less honorable we treat with special honor. And the parts that are unpresentable are treated with special modesty, ²⁴ while our presentable parts need no special treatment. But God has put the body together, giving greater honor to the parts that lacked it, ²⁵ so that there should be no division in the body, but that its parts should have equal concern for each other. ²⁶ If one part suffers, every part suffers with it; if one part is honored, every part rejoices with it.

²⁷ Now you are the body of Christ, and each one of you is a part of it.

STICK TOGETHER

Most regions of the world are familiar with the amazing phenomenon of snow. Snowflakes are beautiful, uniquely crafted ice crystals. Individual snowflakes are fragile, and they quickly melt if they land on your 98-degree warm hand.

Yet *together* snowflakes create an unstoppable force. They can shut down major cities when they cover roads or weigh down power lines. At the same time, they create incredible beauty that inspires photography and art. And exciting opportunities for skiers and snowboarders. And inexpensive fun for people building snow people, snow animals, and snow forts; for snowball "competitions" and sledding hills. All this happens because snowflakes stick together.

We who follow Jesus Christ are similar. Each of us is beautiful, uniquely crafted, and fragile when operating independently. But together with others we can be unstoppable. We can demonstrate God's power and beauty; we can feed the hungry, care for orphans, create music, build homes, take care of the planet, spread the gospel, and so much more. None of us are intended to live in isolation—together we become a great force for God in doing His work.

Who are the people in your faith community, the ones you can call at any time? Take time to thank God for these amazing people.

DAY 63

¹ Shout for joy to the LORD, all the earth.
²Worship the LORD with gladness;
come before him with joyful songs.
³ Know that the LORD is God.
It is he who made us, and we are his;
we are his people, the sheep of his pasture.

⁴ Enter his gates with thanksgiving
and his courts with praise;
give thanks to him and praise his name.
⁵ For the LORD is good and his love endures forever;
his faithfulness continues through all generations.

YOU'RE A DEARLY LOVED ORIGINAL

Each of us is an original work, made personally by God. God is making you braver, stronger, purer, more peaceful, more loving, less selfish, able to solve problems, courageous enough to reach your life goals, more discerning in recognizing friends—the kind of person you've always wanted to be. How does He know what you want to be? Because He knows you inside and out. And He knows who you are becoming.

Here are a few of the hundreds of Bible promises related to you:

- "It is he who made us, and we are his" (Psalm 100:3).
- "If you declare with your mouth, 'Jesus is Lord,' and believe in your heart that God raised him from the dead, you will be saved" (Romans 10:9).

- "He who began a good work in you will carry it on to completion until the day of Christ Jesus" (Philippians 1:6).
- "God will meet all your needs according to the riches of his glory in Christ Jesus" (Philippians 4:19).
- "If any of you lacks wisdom, you should ask God, who gives generously to all without finding fault, and it will be given to you" (James 1:5).
- God's "unfailing love continues forever and his faithfulness continues to each generation" (Psalm 100:5 NLT).

"Forever" goes in both directions. God has always loved you, and He will stick with you to the end. He sees you—the good and the bad—and loves you anyway. He will never give up on you. God's complete love for you is a good reason to have joy and to "come before him with joyful songs" (v. 2)!

?

How do you respond to the fact that God knows your thoughts, dreams, faults, and strengths, and is still going to stay with you?

¹² And now, Israel, what does the LORD your God ask of you but to fear the LORD your God, to walk in obedience to him, to love him, to serve the LORD your God with all your heart and with all your soul, ¹³ and to observe the LORD's commands and decrees that I am giving you today for your own good?

¹⁴ To the LORD your God belong the heavens, even the highest heavens, the earth and everything in it. ¹⁵ Yet the LORD set his affection on your ancestors and loved them, and he chose you, their descendants, above all the nations—as it is today. ¹⁶ Circumcise your hearts, therefore, and do not be stiff-necked any longer. ¹⁷ For the LORD your God is God of gods and Lord of lords, the great God, mighty and awesome, who shows no partiality and accepts no bribes.

FEAR AND LOVE

This is the tale of two schoolteachers. One was loved by his class, because the students could do whatever they wanted. He was laid-back and unconcerned. They didn't need to listen to him because he never gave detentions! The other was feared by his class, because the students were always under his watchful eye. He was strict and vigilant. He kept control, maintained discipline, and kept the students focused on their work. But by the end of the school year, the students preferred the strict teacher. He got good results out of his students and treated everyone fairly. And that classroom was much safer because nobody hurled insults (or pencils) that the teacher ignored.

Deuteronomy 10 says that following God needs both fear and love. In verse 12, we are told "to fear the LORD your God" and "to love him." Why?

To fear the Lord God is to give Him the highest respect. It's not about being terrified of Him. It's about respecting who He is—God!—and the authority He has over everything. A right kind of fear happens when we understand that he's all-powerful and we're not; He's all-knowing and we're not; He's present everywhere—and we're not. And we love that about Him! We aren't bullied into loving Him; we love Him because of who He is. Because of His great power, we can trust Him and feel safe under His watchful eye, and that makes us want to serve and obey Him.

How do fear and love go together in the way we relate to God? Why—in relationships with people—is some fear destructive, and not anything like the fear of God?

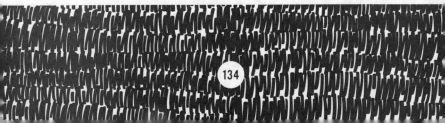

READ 1 KINGS 12:1–8 NLT

¹ Rehoboam went to Shechem, where all Israel had gathered to make him king. ² When Jeroboam son of Nebat heard of this, he returned from Egypt, for he had fled to Egypt to escape from King Solomon. ³ The leaders of Israel summoned him, and Jeroboam and the whole assembly of Israel went to speak with Rehoboam. ⁴ "Your father was a hard master," they said. "Lighten the harsh labor demands and heavy taxes that your father imposed on us. Then we will be your loyal subjects."

⁵ Rehoboam replied, "Give me three days to think this over. Then come back for my answer." So the people went away.

⁶ Then King Rehoboam discussed the matter with the older men who had counseled his father, Solomon. "What is your advice?" he asked. "How should I answer these people?"

⁷ The older counselors replied, "If you are willing to be a servant to these people today and give them a favorable answer, they will always be your loyal subjects."

⁸ But Rehoboam rejected the advice of the older men and instead asked the opinion of the young men who had grown up with him and were now his advisers.

Read the whole passage: 1 Kings 12:1–20.

WISE ADVICE

A newspaper in Singapore printed life lessons from eight senior citizens. It opened by explaining that though aging brings challenges to mind and body, it can fill a person with wisdom. Older people have had more time to see the results of certain choices.

This wisdom doesn't come automatically—any more than knowledge comes to a high school student just by going to class. Older people can choose to become wise or to stay foolish. If they have done the steady work of obeying God and of listening to God day after day, they will have a lot to teach us about life and love.

Rehoboam was a newly crowned king in the Bible who ignored this truth. King Solomon had just died and in 1 Kings 12:3, "the whole assembly of Israel went to Rehoboam" with a request. They asked the new king to lessen the hard labor and heavy taxes Solomon had demanded of them. In return they would loyally serve Rehoboam. At first the young king talked with the elders (v. 6), who agreed that if Rehoboam served the people, the people would serve him in return. They had learned from their experiences with Solomon.

But Rehoboam pushed away the elders' advice and instead followed the foolish words of his friends—"the young men who had grown up with him" (v. 8). These men likely had no experience with leadership but seemed to want power. So Rehoboam made the people work even harder and pay even more taxes, and his bad decision cost him most of his kingdom.

We all need advice that comes from years of experience, especially from those who have walked with God for many years. Think of everything that God has already taught them that could save us from making mistakes! Then spend time with them and listen to what they have to say.

—————————— ? ——————————

When do you want the wisdom of older people? When do you want the advice of younger people? How do you decide which ones to listen to?

¹⁰ God, for whom and through whom everything was made, chose to bring many children into glory. And it was only right that he should make Jesus, through his suffering, a perfect leader, fit to bring them into their salvation.

¹¹ So now Jesus and the ones he makes holy have the same Father. That is why Jesus is not ashamed to call them his brothers and sisters. ¹² For he said to God,

"I will proclaim your name to my brothers and sisters.
    I will praise you among your assembled people."

¹³ He also said,

"I will put my trust in him."
    that is, "I and the children God has given me."

¹⁴ Because God's children are human beings—made of flesh and blood—the Son also became flesh and blood. For only as a human being could he die, and only by dying could he break the power of the devil, who had the power of death. ¹⁵ Only in this way could he set free all who have lived their lives as slaves to the fear of dying.

¹⁶ We also know that the Son did not come to help angels; he came to help the descendants of Abraham. ¹⁷ Therefore, it was necessary for him to be made in every respect like us, his brothers and sisters, so that he could be our merciful and faithful High Priest before God. Then he could offer a sacrifice that would take away the sins of the people. ¹⁸ Since he himself has gone through suffering and testing, he is able to help us when we are being tested.

SIN HURTS PEOPLE

When we say something unkind and see pain on a friend's face, it hurts. When we mess up again and again, it hurts. When we don't help a sibling, it hurts. When others ignore or make fun of us, it hurts. No matter what sin looks like or whose fault it is, sin always hurts.

Think about a time when your guilt or pain felt so heavy that you didn't think you could move. Now try to imagine the heaviness of everyone's sin. What would it feel like to carry the hurt and shame of everything your family, your school, your state, your country—the whole world—has ever done wrong! Throughout history!

Thinking about it like that, it's no surprise that the weight of all this sin began pressing heavily on Jesus the night before His execution (Matthew 26:36–44). But His love kept Him going. His strength bore it and His power beat it. Thanks to Jesus's death and resurrection, we can know without a doubt that sin will not and cannot win.

?

When have you felt the weight of sin? Have you allowed Jesus to take away your sin? How can you show that you appreciate what His sacrifice did for you?

138

¹⁴ Encourage the disheartened, help the weak, be patient with everyone. ¹⁵ Make sure that nobody pays back wrong for wrong, but always strive to do what is good for each other and for everyone else.

¹⁶ Rejoice always, ¹⁷ pray continually, ¹⁸ give thanks in all circumstances; for this is God's will for you in Christ Jesus.

¹⁹ Do not quench the Spirit. ²⁰ Do not treat prophecies with contempt ²¹ but test them all; hold on to what is good, ²² reject every kind of evil.

²³ May God himself, the God of peace, sanctify you through and through. May your whole spirit, soul and body be kept blameless at the coming of our Lord Jesus Christ. ²⁴ The one who calls you is faithful, and he will do it.

SHOULD I SPEAK UP?

During a heated soccer game between two high school rivals, the home team kicked the ball into the goal. The ball hit the back of the net—and went straight through a hole and out the other side. The referee, who didn't see the ball enter the goal, spotted the ball behind the net and concluded there had been no score. The away-team coach saw the goal and spoke up to confirm the home-team coach's claim that his team had scored. He could have kept quiet. The referee awarded the goal. The away team lost the game 3–2.

It's easy to speak up when we want to get our way, but this competing coach obeyed the Bible's command to "always strive to do what is good for each other and for everyone else" (1 Thessalonians 5:15). Who exactly is "everyone else"? Well, it's more than just our friends or family, or even just people we know. It includes every human, even those on opposing soccer teams. This verse is about doing good even to them, without expecting anything in return (Luke 6:35)—no recognition, no gratitude, no favors.

When we actively do good for others, we're letting God work through us. We're demonstrating that God's love is real and belongs to absolutely everyone.

What does it tell others about God's view of them if you are unkind, mean, or happy to avoid them? How can you show what God's love is really like, even to people you don't get along with?

¹⁹ Therefore, brothers and sisters, since we have confidence to enter the Most Holy Place by the blood of Jesus, ²⁰ by a new and living way opened for us through the curtain, that is, his body, ²¹ and since we have a great priest over the house of God, ²² let us draw near to God with a sincere heart and with the full assurance that faith brings, having our hearts sprinkled to cleanse us from a guilty conscience and having our bodies washed with pure water. ²³ Let us hold unswervingly to the hope we profess, for he who promised is faithful. ²⁴ And let us consider how we may spur one another on toward love and good deeds, ²⁵ not giving up meeting together, as some are in the habit of doing, but encouraging one another—and all the more as you see the Day approaching.

HYGGE

Denmark is one of the happiest countries in the world according to the World Happiness Report. The Danes get through their long, dark winters by meeting up with friends to share a warm drink or a big meal. The word they use for how they feel during these times is *hygge* (hoo-gah).

Hygge helps them cope with the tiny quantity of sunlight they experience during winter. By sitting around a table with friends and family, they find themselves refreshed and energized.

The writer of Hebrews encourages this critical practice of meeting together. Hanging out with God's people will keep us going. We all encounter difficult days—with challenges far worse than the weather—that make it hard to keep going. We also experience happy days that we want to talk about and to celebrate.

Even though Jesus has secured us with God forever, we still struggle with problems of this world: cruelty, temptation, death, disease, disability, anguish, and more. We also experience guilt and shame, some of which is real and some of which is not. By hanging out with our church family, we can encourage one another through tough times. When we're sharing each other's company and showing interest, we're able to "spur one another on toward love and good deeds" (Hebrews 10:24).

Spending time with friends actually means we'll rank higher on the happiness scale. And it will keep us going with Jesus when all we want to do is give up.

Talk with God about connections He wants you to make. Which people can you meet up with—friends, youth group, family—so you can help each other through both hard times and happy times?

GALATIANS 6:7-10

⁷ Do not be deceived: God cannot be mocked. A man reaps what he sows. ⁸ Whoever sows to please their flesh, from the flesh will reap destruction; whoever sows to please the Spirit, from the Spirit will reap eternal life. ⁹ Let us not become weary in doing good, for at the proper time we will reap a harvest if we do not give up. ¹⁰ Therefore, as we have opportunity, let us do good to all people, especially to those who belong to the family of believers.

PAIN TO GAIN

During a summer football camp, the team coaches wore T-shirts with a message. The words read: "Each day you must choose: the pain of hard work or the pain of regret." They wanted to get their team to put in as much effort as possible each day!

Hard work and discipline are often things we don't want to have to endure. But we do them more willingly if we know there will be a good result. In sports, in band, in competitions, in school, in relationships, and in the rest of life, the short-term pain of effort is often the only way to do better in the long run.

Too often we're left saying, "What if," "If only," and "I should've." That's the pain of regret. Anyone who says they have no regrets is not likely being honest. It's painful to look back at our choices and see things we could have done better and problems we could have avoided. Proverbs 10:5 says, "He who gathers crops in summer is a prudent son, but he who sleeps during harvest is a disgraceful son." If we avoid hard work we can end up embarrassing ourselves or feeling ashamed.

What specific hard work do you need to do today? What regret could you avoid by doing this hard work? Besides just avoiding regret, you'll be able to share in and celebrate the good that comes from working hard—winning the game, acing the test, enjoying the food, receiving a thank-you, seeing a friend meet Jesus. What will you enjoy later from the hard work you do today?

———————————— ? ————————————

Just between you and God, what are some of your regrets?
What have you learned from your regrets?

¹ Keep on loving one another as brothers and sisters. ² Do not forget to show hospitality to strangers, for by so doing some people have shown hospitality to angels without knowing it. ³ Continue to remember those in prison as if you were together with them in prison, and those who are mistreated as if you yourselves were suffering.

⁴ Marriage should be honored by all, and the marriage bed kept pure, for God will judge the adulterer and all the sexually immoral. ⁵ Keep your lives free from the love of money and be content with what you have, because God has said,

> "Never will I leave you;
> never will I forsake you."

⁶ So we say with confidence,

> "The Lord is my helper; I will not be afraid.
> What can mere mortals do to me?"

⁷ Remember your leaders, who spoke the word of God to you. Consider the outcome of their way of life and imitate their faith. ⁸ Jesus Christ is the same yesterday and today and forever.

NEVER ALONE

People in England love "the Beautiful Game." Millions support the Liverpool Football Club in the English Premier League. At their matches at Anfield, Liverpool fans join together to sing "You'll Never Walk Alone." It's something special to hear fifty thousand fans sing such a powerful song together! That song is important to Liverpool soccer fans and players.

Each one of us wants to belong and to know we won't be left alone. Belonging is a good and godly need given to us by God, and He knows just how to make it happen. God made us to live as part of His family, with people around us to look out for us, to do life with us, and to comfort us when things are hard. You and I are part of God's look-out-for-people strategy.

But living that out in real life is not easy, what with getting cut from sports teams or being attacked by unkind remarks. The solution is to go on the offensive, to be the one who creates belonging. Physically open your circle to welcome someone to the conversation. Say hello and mean it with your eyes as well as your words. Affirm someone for sharing a great idea. Support the people who did make the team. Invite someone else's opinion or creative skills.

God has promised: "Never will I leave you; never will I forsake you" (Hebrews 13:5). These are not just words from a song to make us feel better. They are words spoken by God to us. It is the promise of God himself to His children. All His children. He is here—and He isn't going away.

Loneliness will come, even to Christians. When that happens, look around for someone who needs you to help them belong. With Jesus, neither of you will ever walk alone.

—————————— ? ——————————

When have you felt lonely and someone else helped you feel included? How can you be the one to create belonging for someone else this week?

JAMES 1:13-22

¹³ When tempted, no one should say, "God is tempting me." For God cannot be tempted by evil, nor does he tempt anyone; ¹⁴ but each person is tempted when they are dragged away by their own evil desire and enticed. ¹⁵ Then, after desire has conceived, it gives birth to sin; and sin, when it is full-grown, gives birth to death.

¹⁶ Don't be deceived, my dear brothers and sisters. ¹⁷ Every good and perfect gift is from above, coming down from the Father of the heavenly lights, who does not change like shifting shadows. ¹⁸ He chose to give us birth through the word of truth, that we might be a kind of firstfruits of all he created.

¹⁹ My dear brothers and sisters, take note of this: Everyone should be quick to listen, slow to speak and slow to become angry, ²⁰ because human anger does not produce the righteousness that God desires. ²¹ Therefore, get rid of all moral filth and the evil that is so prevalent and humbly accept the word planted in you, which can save you.

²² Do not merely listen to the word, and so deceive yourselves. Do what it says.

HUMBLY ACCEPT

Think for a moment about this sentence from James 1:21: "humbly accept the word planted in you." Perhaps you are trying to make a big decision, or maybe you are struggling to figure out how to handle a situation. As you read "humbly accept the word," it might help you decide: *I don't need to read another book, hear another speaker, or get more advice. I just need to do what the Bible says.* Sometimes we overthink situations when God has already said everything we need to know.

It's not that asking for advice is wrong. We almost always need it to understand what God is telling us to do. But sometimes, we already know. James wrote to Christians when he gave these straightforward instructions: "Get rid of all moral filth and the evil that is so prevalent and humbly accept the word planted in you, which can save you. Do not merely listen to the word, and so deceive yourselves. Do what it says" (vv. 21–22).

The original word used in this verse translated *accept* means to deliberately and readily receive what is offered. For instance, getting rid of the evil might mean you need to stop criticizing teachers and friends. Or blowing up at your kid brother. Maybe you've been trying to impress people by whipping out funny sarcastic insults. People laugh and you feel clever. But the person you've insulted may just feel . . . insulted . . . even if she laughs. You know God wants you to stop. You just need to "accept the word" that says not to let corrupt talk come from our mouths (Ephesians 4:29).

In all things: Humbly accept the Word.

?

What are some of your favorite ways to delay doing the right thing? How do you talk yourself out of doing what you know you should do?

[1] The LORD said to Moses, "Speak to the entire assembly of Israel and say to them: . . .

[11] "Do not steal.

"Do not lie.

"Do not deceive one another.

[12] "Do not swear falsely by my name and so profane the name of your God. I am the LORD.

[13] "Do not defraud or rob your neighbor.

"Do not hold back the wages of a hired worker overnight.

[14] "Do not curse the deaf or put a stumbling block in front of the blind, but fear your God. I am the LORD.

[15] "Do not pervert justice; do not show partiality to the poor or favoritism to the great, but judge your neighbor fairly.

[16] "Do not go about spreading slander among your people.

"Do not do anything that endangers your neighbor's life. I am the LORD.

[17] "Do not hate a fellow Israelite in your heart. Rebuke your neighbor frankly so you will not share in their guilt.

[18] "Do not seek revenge or bear a grudge against anyone among your people, but love your neighbor as yourself. I am the LORD."

ZERO TOLERANCE

As a part of trying to prevent bullying, some schools have adopted a zero-tolerance approach to gossiping. While it's not clear how they can stop the students from talking behind each other's backs, they do come down hard on anyone they catch gossiping. The schools say they want their students to talk face-to-face if they have a problem with each other. That way things can get sorted out quickly. It sounds like a good idea.

In the Old Testament, God told His people about His own zero-tolerance approach to gossiping (Leviticus 19:16). There was no room for His people to spread lies or rumors or slander of any kind about each other. King Solomon also warned that saying nasty things about others would have horrible effects. It destroys trust (Proverbs 11:13), breaks friendships (16:28; 17:9), gives everyone a bad reputation (25:9–10), and just leads to more and more fighting and arguing (26:20–22). Once gossiping has started, it's very hard to stop it from causing pain and anger.

Here's an idea: Ask God to help you stop saying hurtful things about others. Every time. Let His Spirit set a guard over your mouth, and ask Him to show you how to share the good things you know instead of the rumors you've heard.

And yes, it's still gossip even when it's true.

?

What is your instinct when you hear gossip at your school or church? How do you think your friends would react if you didn't take part in it? Who would like it?

⁶ The wolf will live with the lamb,
>   the leopard will lie down with the goat,
the calf and the lion and the yearling together;
>   and a little child will lead them.
⁷ The cow will feed with the bear,
>   their young will lie down together,
>   and the lion will eat straw like the ox.
⁸ The infant will play near the cobra's den,
>   and the young child will put its hand into the viper's nest.
⁹ They will neither harm nor destroy
>   on all my holy mountain,
for the earth will be filled with the knowledge of the LORD
>   as the waters cover the sea.

UNLIKELY FRIENDS

You may have seen YouTube videos of unlikely animal friendships—like the puppy and piglet who go everywhere together and the giraffe and ostrich who have decided they are best friends!

While surprising to us, friendships across species may have been normal in the garden of Eden. Adam and Eve lived peacefully together with God, with each other, and with the animals (Genesis 1:30). But this peace shattered when Adam and Eve disobeyed God (3:21–23). Now, both in our relationships with people and in the way the world works, we experience struggle and conflict. We make this worse with our own sins. We make this better with our obedience to God shown through love for people.

Isaiah tells us that, one day, "the wolf will live with the lamb, the leopard will lie down with the goat, the calf and the lion and the yearling together" (11:6). Many Christians think this verse is about the day when Jesus will come again to rule. When He returns, there will be no more conflicts and "no more death . . . or pain, for the old order of things has passed away" (Revelation 21:4). On that new earth, everything will be made peaceful again. People of every nation will join together to praise God (7:9–10; 22:1–5).

One day God will bring back perfect peace. While we still wait for that peace to fully come, we can create peaceful conditions with the people we know. We can forgive, love, and maybe even form unlikely—and fun—friendships.

?

What surprising—or bizarre—animal friendship would you like to see on the new earth? What wild animal would you most like for a pet?

DAY 74

ROMANS 8:31-39

³¹ What, then, shall we say in response to these things? If God is for us, who can be against us? ³² He who did not spare his own Son, but gave him up for us all—how will he not also, along with him, graciously give us all things? ³³ Who will bring any charge against those whom God has chosen? It is God who justifies. ³⁴ Who then is the one who condemns? No one. Christ Jesus who died—more than that, who was raised to life—is at the right hand of God and is also interceding for us. ³⁵ Who shall separate us from the love of Christ? Shall trouble or hardship or persecution or famine or nakedness or danger or sword? ³⁶ As it is written:

> "For your sake we face death all day long;
>   we are considered as sheep to be slaughtered."

³⁷ No, in all these things we are more than conquerors through him who loved us. ³⁸ For I [Paul] am convinced that neither death nor life, neither angels nor demons, neither the present nor the future, nor any powers, ³⁹ neither height nor depth, nor anything else in all creation, will be able to separate us from the love of God that is in Christ Jesus our Lord.

DOES GOD OWE YOU?

Sometimes we think that the more energy and time we give God, the more good stuff He will give us in return. When troubles come, we might get angry. Or when good things come, we might have a false sense of security, thinking that the good things are what we can expect from God. But we all know people who love Jesus and have suffered excessively or unfairly. Victims of drunk drivers, medical malpractice, or natural disasters. People who have lost jobs, lost the people they love, or lost all of their worldly possessions. Worse, we hear about people being enslaved or tortured.

When life is hard and stuff is going wrong, turn to Romans 8:35: "Who shall separate us from the love of Christ? Shall trouble or hardship or persecution or famine or nakedness or danger or sword?" In that one sentence Paul summed up his whole life. He went through many trials, yet somehow he was able to keep trusting that these terrible things—not in any way good in themselves—could not separate him from God's love. He had learned to see past the problems and pain to the loving God who will one day return in victory.

Paul wrote, "I am convinced that . . .[nothing] will be able to separate us from the love of God that is in Christ Jesus our Lord" (vv. 38–39). Confidence like that can keep us going when things don't work out the way we expected them to.

How has God gotten you through a terrible time? How has God gotten you through a wonderful time?

PHILIPPIANS 4:10-19

[10] I [Paul] rejoiced greatly in the Lord that at last you [the church at Philippi] renewed your concern for me. Indeed, you were concerned, but you had no opportunity to show it. [11] I am not saying this because I am in need, for I have learned to be content whatever the circumstances. [12] I know what it is to be in need, and I know what it is to have plenty. I have learned the secret of being content in any and every situation, whether well fed or hungry, whether living in plenty or in want. [13] I can do all this through him who gives me strength.

[14] Yet it was good of you to share in my troubles. [15] Moreover, as you Philippians know, in the early days of your acquaintance with the gospel, when I set out from Macedonia, not one church shared with me in the matter of giving and receiving, except you only; [16] for even when I was in Thessalonica, you sent me aid more than once when I was in need. [17] Not that I desire your gifts; what I desire is that more be credited to your account. [18] I have received full payment and have more than enough. I am amply supplied, now that I have received from Epaphroditus the gifts you sent. They are a fragrant offering, an acceptable sacrifice, pleasing to God. [19] And my God will meet all your needs according to the riches of his glory in Christ Jesus.

FAST FEET

There's a rugby competition called the Six Nations Championship. One year an incident in that annual tournament got some people's attention. One of the French players was injured and had to be taken to the sidelines. As the trainers and sports physicians gathered around him, the camera showed a close-up of his shoes. With a black marker the athlete had written: "Habakkuk 3:19" and "Jesus is the way." Christians who saw this were surprised, but also encouraged, to see him reminding himself to make his walk with Jesus as swift and honorable as possible.

Do you happen to know the Bible verse on that rugby player's shoes? Habakkuk 3:19 says, "The Sovereign LORD is my strength; he makes my feet like the feet of a deer, he enables me to tread on the heights." This verse must have been important for the rugby player, whose whole career was about being his feet! But it's also a verse for all of us, about keeping on keeping on, about relying on God, and about making nimble moves that keep us out of danger.

As followers of Jesus, we all need God's strength in everything we go through. He alone can give us "feet" that "tread on the heights." He alone can give us everything we need for the uncertain and difficult times. He alone knows the way ahead and is with us every step of the way. As Paul tells us: "My God will meet all your needs according to the riches of his glory in Christ Jesus" (Philippians 4:19).

— ? —

How has God given you fast and strong feet when the pressure is greatest? Talk with Him about how to walk the next challenge you're facing.

JOB 26:7-14

[7] He spreads out the northern skies over empty space;
   he suspends the earth over nothing.
[8] He wraps up the waters in his clouds,
   yet the clouds do not burst under their weight.
[9] He covers the face of the full moon,
   spreading his clouds over it.
[10] He marks out the horizon on the face of the waters
   for a boundary between light and darkness.
[11] The pillars of the heavens quake,
   aghast at his rebuke.
[12] By his power he churned up the sea;
   by his wisdom he cut Rahab [a mythical sea monster]
      to pieces.
[13] By his breath the skies became fair;
   his hand pierced the gliding serpent.
[14] And these are but the outer fringe of his works;
   how faint the whisper we hear of him!
   Who then can understand the thunder of his power?

Read Job 38 for more about God's amazing control over His creation.

HANGING ON NOTHING

The Earth's mass is 6.6 sextillion tons. And what supports all that weight? Nothing! Planet Earth spins on its axis at one thousand miles per hour as it hurtles through space in its orbit around the sun. This is hard to grasp as we peacefully explore in the woods, build fragile sandcastles on the beach, or walk up the school steps without falling down!

157

Job, a guy in the Old Testament, was trying to cope with the loss of his children, his health, and his possessions. In the midst of his grief, he affirms God's power and control: "He spreads out the northern skies over empty space," Job said. "He suspends the earth over nothing" (Job 26:7). Job described the clouds that don't break even with heavy water inside them (v. 8). Job describes these things as just "the outer fringe" of God's works (v. 14). All of these examples are just a "faint whisper" of His real power.

Creation couldn't answer Job's questions about why all those bad things happened to him, but it did point him to God the Creator—the only One with strength to give Job the help and hope he needed.

What facts about our planet and galaxy give you a sense of wonder? What is your favorite part of nature and how does it help you appreciate God?

⁴ This is what the LORD says to me:

> "As a lion growls,
>   a great lion over its prey—
> and though a whole band of shepherds
>   is called together against it,
> it is not frightened by their shouts
>   or disturbed by their clamor—
> so the LORD Almighty will come down
>   to do battle on Mount Zion and on its heights.
> ⁵ Like birds hovering overhead,
>   the LORD Almighty will shield Jerusalem;
> he will shield it and deliver it,
>   he will 'pass over' it and will rescue it."

REVELATION 5:5

Do not weep! See, the Lion of the tribe of Judah, the Root of David, has triumphed.

☀ THE LION ☀

The lions in Kenya's Maasai Mara game reserve look harmless if you are seeing them while on a safari. They roll on their backs in the sun. They rub their faces on branches as if trying to comb their manes. They drink quietly from a stream. They walk slowly across the dry ground as if they had all the time in the world. You only see their teeth when they yawn.

But their relaxed appearance isn't the whole picture. The reason they can be so relaxed is likely that they have nothing to fear—they're at the top of the food chain. The lions look lazy, even bored, but they are strong and fierce animals. One roar sends all other animals running for their lives.

Sometimes it seems as if God is lazing about. When we don't see Him at work, we think He's not doing anything. When we hear people make jokes about God and say He's not even real, maybe we wonder why He doesn't defend himself. But God "is not frightened by their shouts or disturbed by their clamor" (Isaiah 31:4). He has nothing to fear. One roar from Him and the world will shake! And He will stay at the top of the food chain. Nothing will triumph over Him.

God as a lion is only one of His images in the Bible. He's also our rock, our hiding place, even a hen who gathers us chicks under His wings (Luke 13:34). How do these images help you in figuring out God's role in your life?

_____ ? _____

What does it mean to you that Jesus is described as a lion in the Bible? What other images of God do you like?

[7] The LORD said, "I have indeed seen the misery of my people in Egypt. I have heard them crying out because of their slave drivers, and I am concerned about their suffering. [8] So I have come down to rescue them from the hand of the Egyptians and to bring them up out of that land into a good and spacious land, a land flowing with milk and honey—the home of the Canaanites, Hittites, Amorites, Perizzites, Hivites and Jebusites. [9] And now the cry of the Israelites has reached me, and I have seen the way the Egyptians are oppressing them. [10] So now, go. I am sending you to Pharaoh to bring my people the Israelites out of Egypt."

[11] But Moses said to God, "Who am I that I should go to Pharaoh and bring the Israelites out of Egypt?"

[12] And God said, "I will be with you. And this will be the sign to you that it is I who have sent you: When you have brought the people out of Egypt, you will worship God on this mountain."

[13] Moses said to God, "Suppose I go to the Israelites and say to them, 'The God of your fathers has sent me to you,' and they ask me, 'What is his name?' Then what shall I tell them?"

[14] God said to Moses, "I AM WHO I AM. This is what you are to say to the Israelites: 'I AM has sent me to you.'"

[15] God also said to Moses, "Say to the Israelites, 'The LORD, the God of your fathers—the God of Abraham, the God of Isaac and the God of Jacob—has sent me to you.'

"This is my name forever,
      the name you shall call me
      from generation to generation."

WHO AM I?

A Christian had an opportunity to speak at Cambridge University in England. But he just didn't feel smart enough to talk to such clever people. He hadn't been to college. He had no special theological training. He admitted to a close friend, "I do not know that I have ever felt more totally unprepared." He prayed for God's help, and God used him, despite his fear, to share the good news about Jesus with those students.

Moses, the one who eventually led 600,000 men plus families from slavery to freedom across the Red Sea (Exodus 12:37), also felt like he wasn't good enough. When God instructed him to tell Pharaoh to let the people go, Moses asked, "Who am I that I should go to Pharaoh?" (Exodus 3:11). Although Moses may have decided he was not the right person because he was "slow of speech" (4:10), God said, "I will be with you" (3:12).

Knowing he would have to share God's rescue plan with the people of Israel, Moses asked God, "Then what shall I tell them?" God replied, "I AM has sent me to you" (vv. 13–14). That name for God, "I AM," was a reminder to Moses that God is all-powerful and ever-present.

We might also feel we can't do what God has asked or expects of us, but God is the one who supplies the power. He can be trusted.

What tasks seem impossible for you to do this week? Ask Jesus to give you His strength to complete them.

[8] For you were once darkness, but now you are light in the Lord. Live as children of light [9] (for the fruit of the light consists in all goodness, righteousness and truth) [10] and find out what pleases the Lord. [11] Have nothing to do with the fruitless deeds of darkness, but rather expose them. [12] It is shameful even to mention what the disobedient do in secret. [13] But everything exposed by the light becomes visible—and everything that is illuminated becomes a light. [14] This is why it is said:

> "Wake up, sleeper,
>   rise from the dead,
>   and Christ will shine on you."

[15] Be very careful, then, how you live—not as unwise but as wise, [16] making the most of every opportunity, because the days are evil. [17] Therefore do not be foolish, but understand what the Lord's will is. [18] Do not get drunk on wine, which leads to debauchery. Instead, be filled with the Spirit, [19] speaking to one another with psalms, hymns, and songs from the Spirit. Sing and make music from your heart to the Lord, [20] always giving thanks to God the Father for everything, in the name of our Lord Jesus Christ.

EVERY MOMENT MATTERS

Interruptions are nothing new. Most days are peppered with things we didn't expect to happen. Our plans often change. Whether it's a sudden fight with somebody at school, sickness that cancels time with a friend, a rained-out ball game, or a global pandemic, life can be unpredictable.

We think interruptions just slow us down. Have you ever thought that they could actually be God's way of protecting you from some unseen danger? Or that they could be opportunities to show God's love and forgiveness? We're told to make "the most of every opportunity" (Ephesians 5:16), even the ones we're not expecting!

Whatever happens today, you can use it as a way to show care. When that friend time is interrupted by illness, create a 3D card that amazes. When someone fights with you, stay calm so the fight doesn't go anywhere. When the ball game is rained out, let yourself finish that book you haven't had time for. Let's be "very careful" (v. 15) about how we live. Rather than getting annoyed at our interruptions, we can ask God to show us what He wants us to do in them. And thank Him for them!

—————— ? ——————

What little things bring you joy? Why do they make you happy?

[19] My dear brothers and sisters, take note of this: Everyone should be quick to listen, slow to speak and slow to become angry, [20] because human anger does not produce the righteousness that God desires. [21] Therefore, get rid of all moral filth and the evil that is so prevalent and humbly accept the word planted in you, which can save you.

[22] Do not merely listen to the word, and so deceive yourselves. Do what it says. [23] Anyone who listens to the word but does not do what it says is like someone who looks at his face in a mirror [24] and, after looking at himself, goes away and immediately forgets what he looks like. [25] But whoever looks intently into the perfect law that gives freedom, and continues in it—not forgetting what they have heard, but doing it—they will be blessed in what they do.

[26] Those who consider themselves religious and yet do not keep a tight rein on their tongues deceive themselves, and their religion is worthless. [27] Religion that God our Father accepts as pure and faultless is this: to look after orphans and widows in their distress and to keep oneself from being polluted by the world.

MEGAN'S GLOVES

When Megan was in third grade, she kept coming home from school without her winter gloves. It drove her mom crazy because she had to keep buying new gloves, which the family couldn't afford. One day her mom got really upset and said, "Megan, you've got to be more careful. You can't keep losing your gloves!"

Megan began to cry. Through her tears she told her mom that as long as she kept getting new gloves, she could give hers away to kids who didn't have any.

Later, when Megan was eighteen, her hobbies included volunteering in the community and mentoring inner-city kids. It felt exactly like the kind of things she was supposed to be doing.

Even a child can figure out ways to love God through loving people. Megan saw love as an action, just as James 1:22 stresses: "Do not merely listen to the word, and so deceive yourselves. Do what it says."

After telling his readers to listen to the Bible and do what it says, James offered a practical example of how to give: "look after orphans and widows" (v. 27). It's all about looking out for those who are in real need. It's important to find the ways God wants us to do what the Bible says.

How can you be like Megan to someone today?

— ? —

What do you like about the actions Megan took? What actions are needed in your school? What would your life look like if you kept an eye out for other people?

GALATIANS 2:1-10

[1] Then after fourteen years, I [Paul] went up again to Jerusalem, this time with Barnabas. I took Titus along also. [2] I went in response to a revelation and, meeting privately with those esteemed as leaders, I presented to them the gospel that I preach among the Gentiles. I wanted to be sure I was not running and had not been running my race in vain. [3] Yet not even Titus, who was with me, was compelled to be circumcised, even though he was a Greek. [4] This matter arose because some false believers had infiltrated our ranks to spy on the freedom we have in Christ Jesus and to make us slaves. [5] We did not give in to them for a moment, so that the truth of the gospel might be preserved for you.

[6] As for those who were held in high esteem—whatever they were makes no difference to me; God does not show favoritism—they added nothing to my message. [7] On the contrary, they recognized that I had been entrusted with the task of preaching the gospel to the uncircumcised, just as Peter had been to the circumcised. [8] For God, who was at work in Peter as an apostle to the circumcised, was also at work in me as an apostle to the Gentiles. [9] James, Cephas and John, those esteemed as pillars, gave me and Barnabas the right hand of fellowship when they recognized the grace given to me. They agreed that we should go to the Gentiles, and they to the circumcised. [10] All they asked was that we should continue to remember the poor, the very thing I had been eager to do all along.

PROVERBS 14:31

Whoever oppresses the poor shows contempt for their Maker, but whoever is kind to the needy honors God.

SHOW, NOT JUST KNOW

Statistics are tricky. While numbers give us important information, numbers can numb us to the people those numbers represent. Take this stat, for instance: Every year 9 million people die from hunger and hunger-related illnesses. That's chilling and, for those who have enough to eat, hard to imagine. Millions of children die each year before their fifth birthday, and a third of those deaths are related to hunger and poor nutrition. These staggering numbers represent individuals loved by God and loved by people.

As followers of Jesus, we are called to show God's love by meeting the needs of these hungry persons. Solomon wrote, "Whoever oppresses the poor shows contempt for their Maker, but whoever is kind to the needy honors God" (Proverbs 14:31). We can find creative ways to meet these needs steadily. For example: grow a garden to donate produce; volunteer at a soup kitchen; petition grocery stores to save their expired stock; support your church's community work; and any number of other practical things.

Accepting this responsibility honors God and His concern for persons. And those who are starving might be better able to hear the message of the cross if their stomachs aren't growling.

?

What are new and clever ways to feed and educate the next 9 million people before they die from hunger?

DAY 82

PSALM 77:10-20

¹⁰ Then I thought, "To this I will appeal:
  the years when the Most High stretched out his right
    hand.
¹¹ I will remember the deeds of the LORD;
  yes, I will remember your miracles of long ago.
¹² I will consider all your works
  and meditate on all your mighty deeds."

¹³ Your ways, God, are holy.
  What god is as great as our God?
¹⁴ You are the God who performs miracles;
  you display your power among the peoples.
¹⁵ With your mighty arm you redeemed your people,
  the descendants of Jacob and Joseph.

¹⁶ The waters saw you, God,
  the waters saw you and writhed;
  the very depths were convulsed.
¹⁷ The clouds poured down water,
  the heavens resounded with thunder;
  your arrows flashed back and forth.
¹⁸ Your thunder was heard in the whirlwind,
  your lightning lit up the world;
  the earth trembled and quaked.
¹⁹ Your path led through the sea,
  your way through the mighty waters,
  though your footprints were not seen.

²⁰ You led your people like a flock
  by the hand of Moses and Aaron.

PART OF GOD'S "WE"

At a local farm show, a Border Collie performed a demonstration of how he moved sheep around. The dog's trainer explained that sheep are weak and tend to be helpless, making them easy targets for wild animals. Sheep's main defense is to stick close together in a tight group. "A sheep alone is a dead sheep," the trainer said. "The dog always keeps the sheep together as it moves them forward." And the dog did!

This can help us think of one of the key images the Bible gives us of God: He is our Shepherd and we are His sheep. And as sheep, we Christians need to walk closely together in this dangerous world!

One psalm writer wrote this about the time God rescued the Jewish nation from slavery in Egypt: "He led his own people like a flock of sheep, guiding them safely through the wilderness. He kept them safe so they were not afraid" (Psalm 78:52–53 NLT). As part of God's flock, we are under His guiding, protecting hand while being surrounded by His family—Christians in family, school, and church. We find safety and support when we spend time with other Christians.

As part of God's flock, we also shouldn't think of ourselves as just "me"—we're part of God's "we"! And we need to stick together.

How do caring Christian people protect you? Who would hurt you rather than protect you?

1 CORINTHIANS 3:10–15

¹⁰ By the grace God has given me, I [Paul] laid a foundation as a wise builder, and someone else is building on it. But each one should build with care. ¹¹ For no one can lay any foundation other than the one already laid, which is Jesus Christ. ¹² If anyone builds on this foundation using gold, silver, costly stones, wood, hay or straw, ¹³ their work will be shown for what it is, because the Day will bring it to light. It will be revealed with fire, and the fire will test the quality of each person's work. ¹⁴ If what has been built survives, the builder will receive a reward. ¹⁵ If it is burned up, the builder will suffer loss but yet will be saved—even though only as one escaping through the flames.

A PLACE TO STAND

A visitor to Jamaica was snorkeling with friends in the Caribbean Sea. The boat that had taken the group out into deep water to see the coral and sea life had gone back to shore to pick up others. Unexpectedly, the man began to feel panicky about being in the open water. Finding it hard to control his breathing, he asked his snorkeling friends for help. They held his arms and kept him above the water while he searched for coral reef close enough to the surface to stand on. Once he had a place for his feet to stand on, his breathing calmed down and he was safe.

You may have experienced similar panic about something going on in your life. Maybe exam stress or friend troubles or simply the messiness of everyday life has you struggling for footing. Here are two things that might help. First, ask a parent, teacher at church, or another Christian to pray for you, talk with you, help hold you up in the water (see Ecclesiastes 4:10), and remind you that you are not alone. Second, make sure that where you stand is the only solid rock in life: Jesus Christ (1 Corinthians 3:11).

It's tough to cope with problems on your own, because we're designed to do life with other people. Get some help from others to secure your footing in Jesus.

Then later, you can be that help for another friend who's struggling.

What recent events have led you to feel a bit like you're drowning? Talk with God about the people who could help you. Then talk with God about people He wants you to help.

¹⁴ "Now fear the LORD and serve him with all faithfulness. Throw away the gods your ancestors worshiped beyond the Euphrates River and in Egypt, and serve the LORD. ¹⁵ But if serving the LORD seems undesirable to you, then choose for yourselves this day whom you will serve, whether the gods your ancestors served beyond the Euphrates, or the gods of the Amorites, in whose land you are living. But as for me and my household, we will serve the LORD."

¹⁶ Then the people answered, "Far be it from us to forsake the LORD to serve other gods! ¹⁷ It was the LORD our God himself who brought us and our parents up out of Egypt, from that land of slavery, and performed those great signs before our eyes. He protected us on our entire journey and among all the nations through which we traveled. ¹⁸ And the LORD drove out before us all the nations, including the Amorites, who lived in the land. We too will serve the LORD, because he is our God."

CHOOSE YOUR GOD

There's an online game based on Greek mythology that introduces you to armies, mythological gods, heroes, and quests. To start the game, you go online to register, choose your god, then build your empire.

Wow! "Choose your god." In our everyday lives, we're sometimes tempted to do the same thing. In a game it may not matter what "god" we choose, but in the real world that choice has present, future, and eternal consequences.

To a generation of believers surrounded by the gods of their day, Joshua declared that they must choose their god—but it must not be done in a casual manner. What makes a being worthy of worship is whether it is real, powerful, and good. Joshua announced his choice: "Choose for yourselves this day whom you will serve, whether the gods your ancestors served beyond the Euphrates, or the gods of the Amorites, in whose land you are living. But as for me and my household, we will serve the LORD" (Joshua 24:15).

Today, as in the days of Joshua, there are many options. And many of the worship choices are sneaky. We know about heads-of-religion gods. We know about worshiping a car or money or fame or power. But what about those sneaky gods: worshiping what your boyfriend or girlfriend says you must do, so he or she won't dump you? Or worshiping good grades so much that you will cheat to get them? Or worshiping your own image, afraid people will see your mistakes, so you lie to protect what you want people to think about you? Fake gods are sneaky. Don't be fooled!

?

Can you worship someone or something without realizing it? What kinds of things or people are you tempted to worship? How do you know when it tips from healthy appreciation to unhealthy worship?

PSALM 55:16-19, 22-23

¹⁶ As for me, I [David] call to God,
    and the Lᴏʀᴅ saves me.
¹⁷ Evening, morning and noon
    I cry out in distress,
    and he hears my voice.
¹⁸ He rescues me unharmed
    from the battle waged against me,
    even though many oppose me.
¹⁹ God, who is enthroned from of old,
    who does not change—
he will hear them and humble them,
    because they have no fear of God. . . .

²² Cast your cares on the Lᴏʀᴅ
    and he will sustain you;
he will never let
    the righteous be shaken.
²³ But you, God, will bring down the wicked
    into the pit of decay;
the bloodthirsty and deceitful
    will not live out half their days.

But as for me, I trust in you.

Read the whole passage: Psalm 55.

TO LEAVE IT ALL BEHIND

David seems to be speaking with a sigh: "Oh, that I had the wings of a dove! I would fly away and be at rest" (Psalm 55:6). When life gets to be too much or we've messed up, we totally get that. We wish we could just escape from here and start again!

David wrote freely about the problems he faced. This time it was violence, stirred up by the disloyalty of an old friend (55:8–14). Fear and terror, pain and trembling, anxiety and restlessness overwhelmed David (vv. 4–5). Is it any wonder he wanted to just disappear?

But David chose to keep going. He could not hide from his life and his own choices that had brought him to this place. He talked with God about his problems: "As for me, I call to God, and the LORD saves me. Evening, morning and noon I cry out in distress, and he hears my voice" (vv. 16–17).

Whatever our troubles—loneliness, bullying, poor grades, family confusions, neglect or cruelty from a former friend, persistent illness, disability—they matter to God. We can call out to God. He understands. He will show us what to do. He will send people to help us, or help us think of who we can ask for help. When things get really bad, you or someone you care about may even be tempted to end it all with suicide, or to leave it all behind by running away. Pause a moment. Hear David say, "Cast your cares on the LORD and he will sustain you" (v. 22). Listen. You'll hear at least some silence, but then you'll sense God's prompting to talk to a certain trustworthy person or take a thoughtful action. God will show you.

You are never alone!

?

What makes you want to just escape and start over? Share these details with God, and then wait one day. Then one more day, and one more day, and on, until the situation is managed.

14 "'To the angel of the church in Laodicea write:

These are the words of the Amen, the faithful and true witness, the ruler of God's creation. 15 I know your deeds, that you are neither cold nor hot. I wish you were either one or the other! 16 So, because you are lukewarm—neither hot nor cold—I am about to spit you out of my mouth. 17 You say, 'I am rich; I have acquired wealth and do not need a thing.' But you do not realize that you are wretched, pitiful, poor, blind and naked. 18 I counsel you to buy from me gold refined in the fire, so you can become rich; and white clothes to wear, so you can cover your shameful nakedness; and salve to put on your eyes, so you can see.

19 Those whom I love I rebuke and discipline. So be earnest and repent. 20 Here I am! I stand at the door and knock. If anyone hears my voice and opens the door, I will come in and eat with that person, and they with me.

21 To the one who is victorious, I will give the right to sit with me on my throne, just as I was victorious and sat down with my Father on his throne. 22 Whoever has ears, let them hear what the Spirit says to the churches."

PERSONALIZED CONCERN

It's easy to think of God as a big, angry schoolteacher, looking for anyone to step out of line so He can land them in detention. But that's not what we see in the Bible book of Revelation. In God's letters to the seven churches, we see His personalized concern for people, showing each church which flaws they need to correct and which strengths they need to feed.

Jesus began many of these seven letters by talking about the good things His people had done. This shows us that when we do what is good and right, He sees and is pleased with us.

But Jesus is also concerned about the mistakes we choose. His positive words in these letters are often followed by clear instructions for change. And while it's not fun to hear Him say, "Yet I hold this against you" (Revelation 2:4; see verses 14 and 20), He keeps us from messing up our lives by showing us what needs to be changed.

This brings us to the point—repentance and the courage to change. When God told these churches to turn away from selfishness and back to following Him (the process of repentance), He showed His love. His goal was not to bring these struggling Christians down, but to bring them back to the goodness He had created for them.

Don't miss the fact that each letter ends with a specific promise for the "victorious" (v. 7). God wants to celebrate and reward those who choose well. What's He saying to you today?

？

We can all find someone who will tell us only what we want to hear. Why is it helpful to have someone who will tell you—in a loving way—what is true? How can you find a person like this? Why is it important for that friend to know Jesus?

JOSHUA 1:1-9

[1] After the death of Moses the servant of the LORD, the LORD said to Joshua son of Nun, Moses' aide: [2] "Moses my servant is dead. Now then, you and all these people, get ready to cross the Jordan River into the land I am about to give to them—to the Israelites. [3] I will give you every place where you set your foot, as I promised Moses. [4] Your territory will extend from the desert to Lebanon, and from the great river, the Euphrates—all the Hittite country—to the Mediterranean Sea in the west. [5] No one will be able to stand against you all the days of your life. As I was with Moses, so I will be with you; I will never leave you nor forsake you. [6] Be strong and courageous, because you will lead these people to inherit the land I swore to their ancestors to give them.

[7] "Be strong and very courageous. Be careful to obey all the law my servant Moses gave you; do not turn from it to the right or to the left, that you may be successful wherever you go. [8] Keep this Book of the Law always on your lips; meditate on it day and night, so that you may be careful to do everything written in it. Then you will be prosperous and successful. [9] Have I not commanded you? Be strong and courageous. Do not be afraid; do not be discouraged, for the LORD your God will be with you wherever you go."

MINDLESS PRAYER

Prayer is not a competition, but there are times when we know we should do better at it than we have been doing. When we review our praying, we can see that sometimes our prayers are pretty mindless. We hear ourselves using words and phrases that are more like thoughtless repetitions than they are meaningful things we actually want to discuss with God. Think, for instance, about the phrase "God, be with me."

Do you ever wonder what God thinks when He hears that? After all, the Bible has already promised that God will never leave us!

God made this promise to Joshua just before he led the Israelites into the promised land (Joshua 1:5). The author of Hebrews later included this promise for all Christians: "Never will I leave you; never will I forsake you" (Hebrews 13:5). In both cases, it's clear that God is with us to give us the strength and courage to live for Him—not to live just for ourselves.

Perhaps a better prayer would be something like this: "God, thank you for being with me all the time. Please lead me in the ways you want me to go. Let me know when I'm starting to get off track," or "God, I know that you said you would never leave me, but I'm feeling alone right now. Help me not to doubt that you love me. Thank you for your promises and help me to hold onto them, no matter how I'm feeling."

As you and I live for God, we can be sure He is with us even without our asking. So, let's take our prayer beyond that as we speak with Him each day.

If you're not sure what to pray, tell God what you know is true about Him. Ask for His guidance for whatever you are facing. Thank Him for His faithfulness.

NAHUM 1:3, 7-8

³ The LORD is slow to anger but great in power;
　　　the LORD will not leave the guilty unpunished.
His way is in the whirlwind and the storm,
　　　and clouds are the dust of his feet. . . .

⁷ The LORD is good,
　　　a refuge in times of trouble.
He cares for those who trust in him,
　　　⁸ but with an overwhelming flood
he will make an end of Nineveh;
　　　he will pursue his foes into the realm of darkness.

ONE CITY, TWO STORIES

The book of Jonah could make a great movie. It has wicked enemies Jonah doesn't want to help, it has Jonah running away from God, it has a raging storm at sea, it has Jonah getting swallowed by a big fish, it has God saving Jonah's life, and it has the happy ending of God's rescue of an entire city.

But the sequel—the book of Nahum—might not make such a good film. In the city of Nineveh, the prophet Nahum taught the people about God just as Jonah had, but about one hundred years later. This time, the people of Nineveh showed no interest in giving their lives to God. Because they rejected God, Nahum delivered the unhappy news that God's judgment would come to wipe them out.

Nahum said this to Ninevah: "The LORD is slow to anger but great in power; the LORD will not leave the guilty unpunished" (Nahum 1:3). But Nahum also had words of comfort. He promised: "The LORD is good, a refuge in times of trouble. He cares for those who trust in him" (v. 7). The Ninevites could choose.

Just because people in the city of Ninevah turned to God during Jonah's story, the people a century later didn't get a free pass. The decision to trust God is an individual one that each person makes. Your parents or some friends may love and follow Jesus, but you have to make your own choice. Each person must choose to trust Jesus for himself or herself, or to say, "No thanks, that's not for me." And when someone says no to God, that's not a good story.

Are you more motivated by God's judgment or by His mercy? When might you need each?

⁹ I, John, your brother and companion in the suffering and kingdom and patient endurance that are ours in Jesus, was on the island of Patmos because of the word of God and the testimony of Jesus. ¹⁰ On the Lord's Day I was in the Spirit, and I heard behind me a loud voice like a trumpet, ¹¹ which said: "Write on a scroll what you see and send it to the seven churches: to Ephesus, Smyrna, Pergamum, Thyatira, Sardis, Philadelphia and Laodicea."

¹² I turned around to see the voice that was speaking to me. And when I turned I saw seven golden lampstands, ¹³ and among the lampstands was someone like a son of man, dressed in a robe reaching down to his feet and with a golden sash around his chest. ¹⁴ The hair on his head was white like wool, as white as snow, and his eyes were like blazing fire. ¹⁵ His feet were like bronze glowing in a furnace, and his voice was like the sound of rushing waters. ¹⁶ In his right hand he held seven stars, and coming out of his mouth was a sharp, double-edged sword. His face was like the sun shining in all its brilliance.

¹⁷ When I saw him, I fell at his feet as though dead. Then he placed his right hand on me and said: "Do not be afraid. I am the First and the Last."

RUSHING WATERS

Iguazú Falls in Brazil is one of the greatest waterfalls in the world. The massive falls are amazing! But while most people are impressed with the massive amounts of water that cascade over the falls, there is something else that causes people to stand in awe of the falls. It's the sound. The sound is thunderously powerful—almost as if the visitor were actually inside the sound itself. It makes the observer feel minuscule in comparison.

With that in mind, think about John in Revelation 1. While on the island of Patmos, he saw a vision of Jesus. John gave a powerful description of Jesus. One aspect he included was that Jesus's "voice was like the sound of rushing waters" (v. 15).

The idea of being overcome with the thunderous sound of Iguazú can help us here. As we realize that those mighty waters can make us think of our own smallness, we can better understand why John fell at the feet of Christ (v. 17).

Maybe that description will help you think about the awesomeness of being with Jesus and lead you to follow John's example of worshiping Him with everything you've got!

—————————— ? ——————————

What experience with nature has taught you about the character of God?

DANIEL 1:3–8, 17

³ Then the king ordered Ashpenaz, chief of his court officials, to bring into the king's service some of the Israelites from the royal family and the nobility—⁴ young men without any physical defect, handsome, showing aptitude for every kind of learning, well informed, quick to understand, and qualified to serve in the king's palace. He was to teach them the language and literature of the Babylonians. ⁵ The king assigned them a daily amount of food and wine from the king's table. They were to be trained for three years, and after that they were to enter the king's service.

⁶ Among those who were chosen were some from Judah: Daniel, Hananiah, Mishael and Azariah. ⁷ The chief official gave them new names: to Daniel, the name Belteshazzar; to Hananiah, Shadrach; to Mishael, Meshach; and to Azariah, Abednego.

⁸ But Daniel resolved not to defile himself with the royal food and wine, and he asked the chief official for permission not to defile himself this way. . . .

¹⁷ To these four young men God gave knowledge and understanding of all kinds of literature and learning. And Daniel could understand visions and dreams of all kinds

DANIEL 12:3

Those who are wise will shine like the brightness of the heavens, and those who lead many to righteousness, like the stars for ever and ever.

Read the whole passage: Daniel 1–2.

⇒ BE A STAR ⇐

If you're far from city lights, the nighttime stars are impressive. They bring light, point the way, and inspire.

What do people stars do? They also bring light by showing the best approaches to do things—by making other people shine or by making a change that brings good for generations. Dream a bit about what kind of star you might like to become, and how you would do it.

A young Jewish prisoner named Daniel rose to stardom. When Daniel and his friends were taken captive by an invading army and sent into another country to live, it was unlikely they would be heard from again. These young people had to begin all over again in a new environment. But they were intelligent and chose to stand out as trustworthy. They also chose to be godly.

Later, when the king over Daniel had a dream that his wise men could not understand or interpret, the frustrated king sentenced his wise men to death. Daniel decided to try interpreting that dream. After Daniel spent the night in prayer, God explained the dream and its meaning to him. Soon Daniel shared with the king what he had learned from God, and the king promoted Daniel to be his advisor (see Daniel 2).

If the story ended there, it would be amazing enough. But some Bible teachers believe Daniel's role in Babylon made people aware of the promised Savior who would be born in Bethlehem. Daniel's teaching may have been the reason that five hundred years later wise men from the East followed a star to find an infant King, worship Him, and return to their country with the good news that God had come to earth (Matthew 2:1–12).

By staying close to God and obeying God in even the little parts of life with Him, you can become a star. The kind that points people to Jesus.

What actions help a person shine in a good way? Through what day-after-day actions would God want you to shine?

AREN'T ALL RELIGIONS REALLY THE SAME?

Suppose that four students were assigned a challenging algebra equation to solve, full of symbols, letters, and brackets. After ten minutes, they had each come up with a different answer. They couldn't all be right . . . could they? Were any of them correct?

The students could have compared their answers and said to each other: *Let's agree to disagree. There's no need to argue about this. I've got the answer that works for me. I'm willing to take my chances. Truth is what you make it.* They each could have felt confident in their personal understanding of this math problem. But they all could have failed the exam if none of them had worked out how to solve that equation properly. There was a correct process to be followed and a right answer to be found. There was real, solid, actual truth.

Maybe it's no big deal to fail a math exam at school when you end up with the wrong answer even after sincere hard work. Maybe your teacher will give you partial credit for your effort or for the parts you did get right. But it's a different thing entirely when an answer is something your life depends on. That's when you need the right answer—the actual truth!

It's no shock to people that most equations have just one right answer. What may be surprising is that religion works in the same way. And our lives do depend on what that truth is.

Q: Why can't different answers all be right?

A: *They have contradictory, mutually exclusive teachings.*

EXAMPLE 1: Buddhism says people are born repeatedly into this world, and through self-control they can be freed from this world and attain Nirvana. Nirvana is a kind of perfect emptiness, free from suffering and the cycle of life. The ability to accomplish this lies within people and their commitment to restrain their desires. Most Buddhists think that the need to believe in God is one of the many weaknesses to overcome in order to attain Nirvana.

Christianity says that people have only one life to live, and their only freedom is found in Jesus Christ. The way to life is to recognize that everyone does wrong and—on their own power—are not able to be good enough for heaven. When people recognize their wrong (sin) and accept Jesus's death and resurrection as payment for their sin, then they can fully enjoy life on this earth and spend eternity with God.

The problem: Buddhism says, "We are the answer to our problems," while Christianity says, "We are the problem and Jesus is the answer." Can both be true and more or less the same thing?

EXAMPLE 2: Islam says that Jesus was a good man, a prophet and messenger of God, that He was born of a virgin, and that He performed miracles. But it denies that Jesus died by crucifixion and that He is the Son of God, the God-man. It is people's good deeds that determine if they will spend eternity with God.

Christianity says Jesus is God himself and that He rose from death never to die again, and that Jesus's death and resurrection are the only way people can spend eternity with God. A person can never be "good enough" to earn a place in heaven.

The problem: Jesus can't be both God *and* not-God. Eternity with God can't be based both on Jesus's death and resurrection *and* denying that Jesus died and rose from death. These answers can't both be right.

EXAMPLE 3: Hinduism says that the spiritual goal of life is to become one with Brahman—the universal soul or supreme being, which everyone has a part of. All forms of life contain the soul, and the soul continues to be reborn in various forms of life (human, animal, plant) until it is released from the cycle of rebirth through devotion and selflessness. All souls will achieve this.

Christianity says that people are created beings, not part of God. Humanity's purpose in life is to glorify God. In life people are given the choice to follow God, and accepting Jesus Christ's gift of salvation is the only way to spend eternity with God.

The problem: People can't be both a part of that essence which is considered God *and* beings created by God. If one of those answers is right, then the other must be wrong.

Q: How can we know that Christianity is the right answer we're looking for?

A: *Jesus's own words about himself don't leave room for believing other answers.*

All religions, including Christianity, have their sacred texts and teachings. But what makes Christianity stand out is its claim that God actually came to earth to make the truth clear to us. This God-man was named Jesus, and He was unlike any other religious leader who has ever lived.

Jesus said He was God: The Jewish historian Josephus (AD 37–ca.100), who didn't follow Jesus, called Jesus the "so-called" God. The Bible makes it clear that Jesus said He was God and that He is "one" with God the Father. Jesus's Jewish listeners were so offended by this that they tried to kill Him, shouting, "You, a mere man, claim to be God" (John 10:33).

Jesus said He was the way to heaven: Jesus told His friends, "I am the way and the truth and the life. No one comes to the Father [to God and therefore heaven, His home] except through me" (John 14:6). Some people think there are many ways to heaven, that all religions get you there in the end, but Jesus taught otherwise.

Jesus said He would die and come back to life: Jesus told His followers that He was going to be executed and that three days later He would come back to life. Many people are revived after death, but they die again. Jesus rose from death never to die again. These followers wrote eye-witness accounts of seeing Jesus after His death and of seeing Him ascend into heaven. The historic record is there that Jesus's followers saw the truth of His claims with their own eyes.

Q: Is there any evidence besides Jesus's own words about himself?

A: *There is evidence from Jesus's friends and from others who would have no reason to lie.*

The way to find what's true is to investigate the evidence. Did four different solutions solve the math problem? The evidence was against it. Did Jesus rise to life? The evidence shows He did.

Jesus's death: Did Jesus really die? Tacitus (ca. AD 56-117), a Roman politician of the same time, wrote that Jesus "suffered the extreme penalty" (crucifixion) under Pontius Pilate. Tacitus was not a Christian and was not sympathetic toward Christians—he was just stating the historical fact that Jesus was put to death. This is one of the most accepted facts in Christian history.

The empty tomb: Jesus's body was put in a tomb with a huge boulder rolled over the entrance and Roman guards stationed outside. After a couple of nights, the tomb was empty—a fact everyone agreed to at the time. The authorities paid the guards to say that Jesus's friends sneaked past them as they slept, rolled the massive boulder away, and stole the body without anyone noticing (Matthew 28:13). Though not admitting the resurrection, they were admitting the tomb was empty.

The eyewitnesses: The Bible tells us that Jesus "was seen by more than five hundred of his followers at one time" (1 Corinthians 15:6 NLT). The people who had met Jesus after His death were still around for questioning when the news of the resurrection was spreading. Yet the Roman Empire and the Jewish authorities never proved the resurrection of Jesus to be fake. Not a single witness cracked under questioning, threats, and torture to say, "We made it up."

Jesus's followers: When Jesus was on trial, Peter (one of His closest friends) denied knowing Him (Matthew 26:69–75). But after Jesus's tomb was empty, Peter boldly stood up in front of the crowds of people who had screamed for Jesus's death, and said, "God has raised this Jesus to life, and we are all witnesses of it. . . . God has made this Jesus, whom you crucified, both Lord and Messiah" (Acts 2:32, 36). Only the Holy Spirit could create a transformation this bold! What had changed to make Peter so brave? He knew that Jesus was alive again.

Records from the time tell us the number of Christians only grew, even though they were hunted, imprisoned, beaten, fed to lions, and killed. Jesus's followers, and those who believed their message, were so convinced by the resurrection that they were ready to die for their belief. Now that's *fearless faith!*